CREATIVE PASTORAL CARE AND COUNSELING SERIES

BECOMING A HEALTHIER PASTOR

Family Systems Theory and the Pastor's Own Family

RONALD W. RICHARDSON

FORTRESS PRESS   MINNEAPOLIS

BECOMING A HEALTHIER PASTOR
Family Systems Theory and the Pastor's Own Family

Cover art © Comstock

Some of the content of chapter 2 is based on a paper by David Freeman and is used with his permission.

Scripture quotations, unless otherwise noted, are from the New Revised Standard Version (NRSV) Bible, copyright © 1989 Division of Christian Education of the National Council of Churches of Christ in the United States of America. Used by permission.

Library of Congress Cataloging-in-Publication Data
Richardson, Ronald W. (Ronald Wayne), 1939–
  Becoming a healthier pastor : family systems theory and the pastor's own family /
Ronald W. Richardson.
    p. cm.—(Creative pastoral care and counseling series)
  Includes bibliographical references.
  ISBN 978-0-8006-3639-5
  1. Pastoral psychology. 2. Clergy—Family relationships. 3. Systemic therapy
(Family therapy) I. Title. II. Series.
  BV4012.R48 2004
  253'.2—dc22
                                        2004018094

The paper used in this publication meets the minimum requirements of American National Standard for Information Sciences—Permanence of Paper for Printed Library Materials, ANSI Z329.48-1984.

Manufactured in the U.S.A.

CONTENTS

EDITOR'S FOREWORD

In a previous book, *Creating a Healthier Church*, Ron Richardson focused on actions that lead to more emotionally positive relationships in congregations. Using the family systems theory of Murray Bowen as a foundation, Richardson conveyed that the dynamics of relationships in churches ". . . are based in cultural, structural communication, decision, and economic systems. These systems are fairly easy to change if necessary. The system most difficult to change is the emotional system" (p. 29). In *Creating a Healthier Church* Richardson described two churches that meet a similar situation within the church in two different ways. In *Becoming a Healthier Pastor* Richardson expands upon his concern about creating healthier churches, now focusing specifically on pastors and what they can do within themselves and in their relationships to improve relationships in the church.

Becoming a Healthier Pastor opens with the story of Pastor Jean Anderson and her response to the death of one of her parishioners. She finds herself in the center of a tug-of-war—stretched by her own family tensions, the need to write Sunday's sermon, phone calls from several church members who are not pleased with her recent sermons, and preparations for the evening's board meeting. Most of us can relate to her situation.

Richardson uses this typical day in the life of one pastor to focus on the pastor's emotional development and how remarkably this development can affect the ways in which clergypersons carry out their ministry. It is surprising that more writers have not attempted to do what Richardson here does so well: to focus on the emotional life of pastors and how they relate to others in the church. The plain fact is that the majority of what pastors do involves their relationships and emotional systems. The church is a community of relationships, and how the leader relates is rather critical; how the minister balances individuality and relatedness is decisive.

The book is about honoring family. The author believes that we can benefit from reflection on our family of origin and the generations that preceded it as a resource in our own development as individuals, as religious persons, as clergy. In the core of the book Richardson looks at the minister's own family and its impact on all pastoral relationships, even using his own family as an example.

If you have not read his previous work from Fortress Press, read *Becoming a Healthier Pastor* now and then go back and read *Creating a Healthier Church*. As a pair, the two works will enrich the reader with a wealth of wisdom that Richardson brings to the rich and complex relationships that make up congregational ministry.

It gives me great pleasure to write a foreword for such an outstanding book by a former student. Of course I would like to claim that at least a portion of what Ron Richardson has achieved is due to our work together some thirty years ago. But reality interrupts; I realize that the wisdom demonstrated in *Becoming a Healthier Pastor* comes from his years of study and practice as a pastoral caregiver. Indeed, I am struck by the amount that I can learn from a former student.

This is a good book.

HOWARD STONE

PREFACE

Honor your father and your mother,
so that your days may be long in the land.
—Exodus 20:12

This commandment is the only one with a promise attached to it. It says that honoring our parents will provide us with longevity. I hear this as a promise of greater health. In general, we in North America have not been very good at following this commandment—not in terms of obeying our parents when we are young children or taking care of them when they are old but in terms of honoring those in our family who have preceded us and whom we may have ignored, rejected, or treated as irrelevant to our current life concerns.

Very few of us as adults have learned to see our family of origin—the family we grew up in that continues the generations of family that preceded us—as a resource to our own physical, emotional, social, and spiritual well-being. In our North American individualistic approach to health, we rarely think of family as contributing to our well-being; rather, we more typically attempt to distance ourselves from them at times as a way to improve our own health. To honor our family, however, is to discover how it can help improve our own lives and well-being. And, strange as it may seem, it is a way to improve our functioning as pastors and as congregational leaders. It is a way to become a healthier pastor.

Bowen family systems theory, an approach to working with families that originated in the field of psychotherapy, has struck a deep chord with many pastors, who have quickly seen its relevance to ministry. I find this remarkable. It is automatic to believe that the tensions in a church can be directly traced to particular, problematic individuals. Blaming individuals for problems in a group is as old as humanity. The fact that so many pastors have been able to get beyond this way of seeing and understanding is truly amazing.

There is no question that every church has particular individuals who refuse to behave the way we would like them to and who seem to cause relationship difficulties in the church. Some pastors become focused on these persons and may negatively describe them and "their problem," but the more that focus happens, the more likely it is that unfruitful, debilitating conflict will develop and perhaps even spread into other areas of church life. This kind of conflict is dispiriting for everyone involved, and usually no one comes out of it feeling good or happy about the outcome.

These particular church members, just as often, blame us the pastors for the problems in the church. We don't behave the way they want us to. Getting beyond this individually focused approach in which we blame them and then react to their blame of us is essential to overcoming the difficulties. It is this focus on the "problem people" as the cause of our personal or congregational tension and anxiety that is the real problem.

Pastors who have become family systems theory practitioners understand that the particular "problem" individuals do not cause our own anxiety and that we do not cause theirs. The difficulties and anxiety are symptoms of a reciprocal process in an emotionally charged congregation in which even we, as leaders, are involved. Successful resolution depends on how we manage ourselves in the congregational emotional process at such times rather than how well we diagnose and manage others. It means managing ourselves in such a way that we do not add to the long-term anxiety in the system but are actually able to help modify it, reduce it, and work toward a solution of the current difficulties.

The congregational emotional system is a powerful influence in the life of the church. It is a major factor in deciding whether and how well congregations fulfill their mission and ministry in the world. When church leaders are more emotionally mature, they can lead more effectively within that emotional system, and the level of functioning of the whole church will be improved, so that it can more faithfully fulfill its calling.

In my book *Creating a Healthier Church* I began with two different congregations facing the same set of stressful conditions on a particular Sunday morning. The pastoral and lay leadership of the congregations had significantly different ways of dealing with the upsetting circumstances they faced. Roy Hanson, the pastor at Valley View Church, was dominated by his reactive feelings. He was so sensitive to whether people were for him or against him, and to their anger at him, that he could not function effectively in the crisis of that Sunday morning. He was totally caught up in the emotionality of those around him and gave back what he got emotionally. He rigidly and tenaciously continued to fight battles with others, and together they kept the church mired down in conflict. This heightened everyone's level of anxiety. Roy could not step outside of the emotionality to become a healthier leader for his congregation. Assuming he continued to function this way for a number of years, his own emotional and physical health would begin to suffer, as would his ministry and career as a pastor.

Bob Stimson, the pastor of Third Church, along with the lay leadership of that church, brought much greater emotional maturity to that same Sunday morning crisis. They were all able to keep their own anxiety at bay and to think more effectively about how to tackle the immediate challenges facing them. They did this in a cooperative and flexible way, displaying an ability to override any emotional reactions they may have had. They didn't need to blame and find fault. They just got on with the job and came out of the experience in pretty good shape. Bob's life was generally better than Roy's, and we can assume that he was a much "healthier" pastor.

We all have some of Roy and some of Bob in us. Each of us has more of one than the other. This book is about how to recognize and come to terms with the part of us that is like Roy and how to develop an emotional maturity more like Bob's. In particular, I describe one specific way of accomplishing this growth that, in terms of Bowen family systems theory language, involves differentiating a self within the emotional system of our family of origin. Our personal progress in working on this project will lead to a higher, healthier level of functioning in nearly every aspect of our lives. And in the process of doing it, the work offers a concrete way to honor our families.

As more and more pastors are becoming interested in family systems theory, many institutions and freestanding groups around the country are teaching it. However, many pastors are becoming involved in the theory without adequate training. They may think of the theory as a set of techniques for doing "tricky" things to a congregation to get it to do what they want. This approach can lead to failure and to disillusionment with the theory.

The personal issues of these pastors may hinder their ability to function effectively as leaders within their congregations, and their misuse of the theory may, in fact, cause them deeper trouble. More training and supervisory opportunities are needed in which pastors can explore not only the theory and its applications but also their personal emotional systems and what patterns they bring to ministry out of their own family of origin. Written material that explores the theory within all the varieties of the pastoral context is also needed.

This book is meant to address some of these concerns. As a follow-up or companion volume to *Creating a Healthier Church*, it begins where that book ended. While writing *Creating a Healthier Church*, I was most aware of a major area I was not addressing: how the growth and development of the pastor's or church leader's own emotional maturity takes place. But space did not allow me to tackle such a large topic within that book.

This current book has one simple premise. Our development and experience within our family of origin is a major but usually hidden component of how we function emotionally within our congregations as pastors. The family we grew up in is the first, most powerful, longest lasting, and nearly indelible training we get for how to be part of a group and to function within it. While our later professional training adds a layer of sophistication and expertise that normally serves us well in ministry, when the level of anxiety goes up in a congregation and we become anxious, we tend to revert to our old family patterns and ways of functioning.

In some cases this will be a good thing, because our family may have taught us, by example, effective ways of dealing with emotionality in groups and in ourselves. We can be sure that Bob Stimson at Third Church came from such a family. But more often, our learned patterns are not appropriate to our role as leaders within our congregations, and we create even more difficulties for ourselves, further raising the level of anxiety and reactivity in the congregation. Individuals who have good success working on themselves within their family of origin will have the best chance of becoming a healthier pastor and more effective leader within their congregation.

ACKNOWLEDGMENTS

Many pastors and students have contributed to the writing of this book. I am deeply grateful that they allowed me to be a part of their journeys and to observe their amazing examples of courage and faith as they did their own family of origin work.

My deepest appreciation goes to three very good friends who served as readers and who offered me valuable advice. First, my old ski buddy Howard Stone, who also happened to be an early supervisor of mine and who is the editor of the Creative Pastoral Care and Counseling series for Fortress Press. Second, I wish to thank Doug Anderson not only for reading and commenting on this text but for being a friendly, caring critic in my life for many years. This book is just another chapter in our ongoing discussions. Third, I wish to thank my colleague and good friend in Vancouver, Randy Frost, who knows so much more about Bowen family systems theory than I do but who will still read my work and offer helpful comments. None of them are responsible for any mistakes in this book, but all three have contributed to its potential usefulness.

I also want to thank Steve and Heather Wilson, of York, England, for their caring and helpful hospitality for my wife and me for five months while we traveled in southern France, where most of this book was written.

Finally, I thank my wife Lois for her companionship and loving helpfulness as I struggle to communicate the ideas in this book in clear language.

NOTE ON CASE HISTORIES

All of the case histories reported in this book accurately reflect actual events. In every case except my own family story, however, identifying characteristics have been changed to protect the confidentiality of the people involved. The stories are used with their permission. On occasion the stories of two or more people have been combined into one for a clearer, more effective presentation of the theory.

INTRODUCTION

THE CHALLENGES OF MINISTRY

At 7:00 a.m., Pastor Jean Anderson got a phone call from the police. One of her parishioners had been killed in a car accident. The police wanted her help in telling the man's wife. As she was getting ready to leave the house, her husband and sixteen-year-old daughter were renewing one of their many recent fights. Both were angry with her for leaving. Her husband was saying he needed her support, and her daughter was accusing her of being unfair and inconsistent in her beliefs for not taking her side in the argument.

When Jean arrived at the parishioner's house, the wife at first refused to believe that her husband was dead. Then she fell apart in tears and collapsed into Jean's arms. Later, at her office, Jean tried to make some headway on doing exegesis for next Sunday's sermon but was interrupted by two phone calls from influential members complaining about last week's sermon. Then she had lunch with a key board member who was under so much stress at work and at home that he couldn't fulfill his board responsibilities and had to resign. As they talked, Jean found herself engaging in a little "escape fantasy" of her own. Making her calls in the afternoon, she returned to visit the wife whose husband had been killed. Then she went to the hospital where she had two parishioners with serious illnesses. One of the parishioners was terminally ill, and the woman's husband, who was at the hospital, was not doing well with the imminent loss and was talking "suicide after she dies."

After dinner that evening, Jean attended a crucial board meeting, in which she was working with opposing sides to resolve a controversial proposal before the board. The meeting was contentious and continued in the parking lot afterward. Jean left the board members, still arguing, at 11:30 p.m., only to go home and find that her daughter had not yet come in. The daughter had been due home at 9:00 p.m.

Some of us can easily identify with a day like this. We have been there. Sometimes we have days even worse than this. How do we get through it? How do we minister to all of our parishioners and continue to be a responsible family member? How do we deal with personal challenges and continue on with ministry in a hopeful way? How do we avoid becoming overwhelmed or burned-out? How do we avoid becoming personally unwell, getting caught up in major conflicts with others, or failing to provide positive leadership in the many critical circumstances of life we all face?

Certain key personal skills allow us to handle these challenges. They make the kind of day described above a little more manageable and more tolerable. These skills involve a central concept of Bowen family systems theory: differentiation of self. They point us in the direction of health and help us to become better pastors and leaders in our church. We all have a certain level of differentiation already; it is what allows us to function as well as we do. But we all can also profit from developing a higher level.

Michael Kerr, the present director of the Bowen Center in Washington, D.C., says that working on differentiation of self is like taking your little sailboat out on to the lake when a storm is brewing, hoping to learn something both about storms and yourself and about how to manage your boat in a storm. The aim of this book is to promote greater differentiation of self, to help us become more of a master of our little ship in the turbulent storms of our relationship life so that we don't get totally lost and can do more than just survive shipwrecks. Differentiation of self offers a more objective way to study the storms in the church and in our personal lives and to develop a perspective on our subjective emotionality within the storms.

MINISTRY AND FAMILY SYSTEMS THEORY

Many books have been written on the practice of ministry. However, very few of these are written from a consistent theoretical point of view. Typically, they bring together a variety of approaches adapted to the author's particular understanding of ministry. While the author may see them as "complementary," these collected approaches are usually not truly consistent with one another in terms of their basic understanding of human functioning. Moreover, because they are so individualistically the author's own formulation, adapting them to our own pastoral work can be difficult.

Even fewer of these books focus on the person of the pastor and how the pastor's own emotional development and experience affect the pastor's ministry. This is remarkable since so much of what we do as pastors focuses on relationships and concerns the emotional experience of parishioners. Experience teaches us, through some unfortunate but dramatic pastoral examples in recent years, that it is not just biblical or theological knowledge or level of piety or amount of prayer or depth of devotion or particular pastoral skills that lead to a successful ministry. Success also has to do with a pastor's level of emotional maturity.

Bowen theory makes two major contributions to our understanding of and practice of ministry. First, it offers a comprehensive theory of human functioning in relationships that applies to nearly all of what we do as pastors, from baptism to death, from individual counseling to social ministry, from administrative work with committees and boards and judicatories to worship and preaching, and from personal Bible study and devotional life to educational ministry. Every aspect of pastoral ministry is informed by the theory.

Urban, suburban, and rural pastors will be able to make good use of the theory for their life and ministry. Family systems theory is not only about individual parishioners, families, congregations, and larger systems in society, but also about our daily practice of ministry. It is about the normal processes of congregational life and our part in them. It is about our strengths and skills as well as our liabilities and problems. And it is about the extraordinary, emotionally challenging situations we face that call for solid critical thinking skills and courageous leadership. It helps us understand why things go well or badly in our ministry.

Second, whatever aspect of ministry we are engaged in, family systems theory understands that we are inevitably involved, at many levels, in the emotional systems of all the people we work with, and that this involvement must—most essentially—include our own emotional system. Very little attention has been paid to how our emotional system, our level of emotional health, and our unresolved attachment with family affect our ministry. Murray Bowen's original work in the field of family therapy led the way by providing a consistent theory of human functioning that included the emotional life of the practitioner. Edwin Friedman continued that work as it applied to ministry. This book is, I hope, another contribution to this way of thinking for ministry.

HEALTH AND MINISTRY

Health is, of course, a relative term. All people, no matter how sick, have some degree of health, or they would not be alive. Only death represents the complete lack of health. Most of us walk around with various levels of health physically and emotionally, and some of us are healthier than the norm and some less. Whatever our own level of health, Bowen theory shows how to strengthen it and to improve our personal and pastoral level of functioning.

In this book the term *health* means specifically the degree of emotional well-being and the level of emotional maturity that allows pastors to engage in the relational aspects of ministry more competently. It is how well pastors can manage themselves while actively relating to church members, especially during times of higher anxiety, so that the goals of ministry can be fulfilled. I do not exclude the possibility that greater emotional well-being and improved social functioning will lead to better physical health as well.

Our level of emotional well-being is, to some extent, tied to that of those around us. Just as some physical diseases are communicable and make their rounds through a social group, so too can emotional distress be circulated within a group such as a congregation. Some people have a stronger emotional immune system and do not become infected, while others are more vulnerable to this distress. As a result, some members of the congregation can end up less healthy than others as the distress settles on them. Often one of those members is the pastor.

THE PASTOR AS PERSON, MINISTER, AND FAMILY MEMBER

Many people try to handle their unresolved attachment to family through their work. It is easy to try to make the church into a substitute family and to address and improve on old family issues there. It is also common to try to resolve old family of origin issues in our new family of creation. In both cases, we try to make these relationships into what our first family was not or to develop what we thought was lacking in that family. These are not so much conscious, intentional acts as they are automatic responses to family experience. Our family of origin experience affects the way we go about our work in the church as well as the kind of family we create in our marriage and the relationship we have with our children.

Our relationships with our partner and our children are generally our most challenging set of relationships. It is easy to focus exclusively on these relationships because issues with our family of origin are regarded as "history" and thus no longer relevant. We believe that our first family's problems have nothing to do with our current problems. For example, we may have written off those family members as "unchangeable."

Some clergy keep a distance not only from their family of origin but also from their nuclear family and instead put most of their life energy into their work. They may find more intimacy with others in their role as pastor than they do as a fully participating member of their own family. It may be that their partner and children don't see them and admire them the way people in the church do, and they need the kind of respect and admiration they get from parishioners. Their church becomes their whole world. Others may feel a certain amount of guilt that drives them to do well in their work, or a sense of inadequacy may make them want to achieve and to demonstrate their competence. These are all family of origin issues at the root.

Some pastors spend so much time dealing with the problems of others and concerns in the church that they don't pay enough attention to their own personal lives and well-being. They can see and minister to the problems of others relatively well but miss their own. They may be totally surprised when they come down with some physical, emotional, or social difficulty that hinders both their work and their ability to minister to others and also be a family member.

Other pastors experience burnout and breakdown, which are often a result of the pastors' position in the emotional system of the church or their family system. This emotional engagement is much more important than the number of hours a pastor works. The emotional overinvolvement and the perception of one's own role as a helper or healer is the real problem.

TOGETHERNESS AND INDIVIDUALITY IN MINISTRY

The understanding of health presented here concerns how well we can balance the basic life forces of togetherness and individuality. It is about the level of our emotional fusion with others and the amount of individuality we have. The more individuality we have (which is not the same as "individualism"), the better we will do at both our work and our family life. The more fused we are into a togetherness-oriented life, the more unbalanced we will be personally and the more difficulties we will encounter in our work and family life.

When the level of anxiety is low in a church, a much greater tolerance of individuality exists. People feel free to be themselves. When anxiety increases in the church, however, pressure increases for everyone to adapt to the others and for everyone to think, feel, and behave the same way. This togetherness pressure can lead to emotional reactivity in some. When this pattern becomes chronic, some people in the system will become less healthy, and one or more symptoms will emerge. Those who can maintain a higher level of individuality will do better at managing their togetherness with others. Greater differentiation of self allows us to be better pastors and family members and to create an appropriate balance in how we divide our time.

The togetherness force is what binds us to one another. It is essential to human community and makes us aware of our need for one another and sympathetic to the unhappy circumstances of others. It is what Paul appeals to in Galatians 6:2 when he asks that we "bear one another's burdens." But it is also what makes us sensitive to approval and criticism, rejection and abandonment, and status within the hierarchy. As the level of anxiety increases in an emotional system, the more pressure there is for absolute conformity to the predominant expectations of those in charge. Free thinking and independent actions are criticized.

Individuality causes us to seek to enhance our ability to think and act according to what makes sense to us. It does not require us to please or convince others before we can act, and it responds less to group pressure to conform. It is often the source of creativity and change and of new solutions to old difficulties. It leads us to define our beliefs and principles as guides for how we will behave. It is this force that leads Paul to say, just a couple of verses later in Galatians, that we must each bear our own burdens and sort out our own solutions to our difficulties. Martin Luther exhibited perhaps the best-known example of individuality in church history when he said, "Here I stand." The more differentiation that exists among the people of a church, the better they will be able to balance togetherness and individuality.

The family of origin is where our ability to balance the relative levels of individuality and togetherness was originally "set." We each have our own thermostatic level or balance, which determines how we manage our personal, family, and professional lives. By the time we leave home, that balance is pretty well established and will remain in place unless we consciously try to change it.

THE APPROACH OF THIS BOOK

Family of origin work is about a way of connecting with the family we grew up in so that we can discover new resources for developing our own life and health. Rather than focusing only on the usual negative or "dysfunctional" aspects of our family life, it offers a way to enhance our skills for increasing greater personal mastery for our lives and for functioning in relation to others both in our family and in our church.

After thirty-five years of doing ministry and training and supervising clergy, I am convinced that those:

- who are most willing to look at their own unresolved emotional attachments within their family of origin,
- who attempt to understand both how their family functions and how they themselves function within that emotional system,
- and who will work on modifying how they function within that system

will become the most effective church leaders and pastors over the long haul.

This kind of growth into greater health is hard work. This is not an easy, quick-fix solution, not a magic bullet that will change things overnight. It does not cure all psychological ills. But it does offer a practical means for achieving a mature personal character and a life of principle based on Christian values.

Seeing families or congregations as systems involves an understanding of people in relationships. When a system is stressed, anxiety often develops. This anxiety can manifest as symptoms in one or more people or relationships. The resulting symptoms can create an imbalance in the system, which may increase anxiety even more, leading to more dramatic efforts to get things rebalanced. Our Christian values and beliefs tend to get lost in the process.

For example, a formerly competent church board president, who is now under some degree of personal stress, may begin to underfunction and "drop the ball" in several key areas. Other board members may then become anxious themselves and focus on his lack of adequate functioning, perhaps getting angry with him. They may even get angry with the pastor for not "straightening him out." If the pastor complies with their wishes and directs a negative focus on the president, confronting him with his underfunctioning, the president may resign or even leave the congregation in anger. Then church members may blame the pastor for not handling the situation well. And on it goes.

The more differentiated people are in the system, the less likely they are to become anxious about the stress of the underfunctioning president, and the more likely they are to respond appropriately to his circumstances. The less differentiated they are, the more their anxiety-based reactions will lead to further disruptions and upset. People may see various individuals as having "problems" and may miss how everyone has participated in the development of the difficulties.

THINKING SYSTEMS AND CHURCH MINISTRY

In preparing for this work, any time spent reading about Bowen family systems theory will be well spent. Because the theory is not easily grasped, it may also help to join a group that discusses and debates the theory. Study of the theory can be a lifelong task that will keep opening new doors of insight at each new level of development.

Understanding the theory and learning to "think systems" is a slow process. Because it differs significantly from our normal individually oriented way of thinking, it takes time and discipline to make the shift. Learning automatically to see the whole emotional system—rather than particular individuals in the system—as the unit of concern and focus, emerges only after much immersion in the theory and its practice. But one day it will just happen, and then you've got it. That is, "you've got it" until the next big crisis hits, when you will probably again have to struggle out of the automatic reactivity of the individual model and renew your picture of the whole.

This book is not about *the* way to do family of origin work. Many ways to do the work exist, and each person's way is unique. No one pattern fits all people and families. This book offers the essential ingredients to do the work, based on the issues and steps people generally experience, but keep in mind that the process varies from person to person.

This book also offers an approach for how pastors can eventually become family coaches to members of their congregations. It is not about how to become a family or marital therapy practitioner. But pastors who know the theory, and who have applied it in their own lives, can become coaches to the members of their congregations and their families.

Part One defines unresolved emotional attachments with the family of origin and shows how these attachments can contribute to some of the daily difficulties we may have in ministry. Part Two considers the goals of the work, discusses some of my own family of origin work, and then describes the essential steps in doing the work. Part Three focuses on pastors being coaches to parishioners in doing their own family work.

IS THIS BOOK FOR YOU? IS THIS A CHALLENGE YOU WANT?

Family of origin work requires a strong sense of personal motivation. Ask the following questions: To what extent do I want to be better connected to family? Do I want to be "present and accounted for" in family, or do I want to maintain distance? Only you can decide how important this is to you.

I don't usually have to tell people that getting reconnected to family can be upsetting. People with lower levels of differentiation, who live life on an emotionally delicate balance, might do best to avoid most aspects of family work. If they happen to have a "supportive" family, then that may be enough. If they decide to pursue the work, then they must go slowly and develop personal resources to fall back on when things don't go as they planned. Having a personal coach will be essential for these people.

Some people don't "feel upset" when they are with their family. They are so emotionally fused with family that it may be like being a part of an engulfing ooze where, amoeba-like, no one moves independently. No one moves unless the whole of the family is in agreement. The "we" of togetherness is stronger than any one person's "I," and to be an individual is almost regarded as a selfish betrayal of the family. It is easier to just submerge into the amoebic ooze. It is difficult to escape this powerful emotional fusion and be a self while also staying connected to family.

However, many people feel so damaged by the families they grew up in that they often want as little to do with them as possible. Any attempt to push these people back toward their family is met with strong reactions and resistance. I understand that because I have been there. While I experienced no great damage within my family, I still wanted to keep my distance from them even as I entered middle age. Having contact with family meant I would only get embroiled in relationships that I had spent my young adult years "escaping." And, as you will see later, I had a pretty "easy" family to deal with. The theory showed me how I could approach my own family and tackle my unresolved issues there, at my own pace, and do the work I needed to do. This made the work less scary, and I thought I could muster the courage to do it. I will tell something of my family story and the work I did in chapter 4.

Whether you are emotionally "overinvolved" or "underinvolved" with your family, the process of differentiating a self within it while staying emotionally connected to it will be a major challenge. It could be more of a challenge than you want at this point in life.

This work is partly about personal courage. I have been privileged as a pastoral counselor to observe people engage in what can only be called "heroic" acts of emotional bravery as they have reconnected with family members in new ways. Some of them have been quite damaged in their families, suffering physical and sexual abuse, or they were the parentified child or the forgotten child or the focused-on child or the "special" child or the "never taken seriously" child or the "never loved" child. One colleague, as a young child and as a teen, had to deal three times with being the person who discovered his mother in her attempts at suicide.

Most of the people I worked with had fairly average families with no huge personal traumas. Still their work called for courage. Deciding to do this work means taking on a major challenge. The timing may not be best for you right now. The effort required can be emotionally demanding. The work takes a lot of personal time, and, if family members live far away, it could also be expensive because of the cost of making regular visits. Generally, visits of two to three days every three to four months are the norm. The work can be done with once-a-year visits, along with use of regular mail and e-mail, but it will proceed more slowly.

However, addressing unresolved emotional attachment with your family of origin will give you a whole new stance on your life, in your own marriage and family, and in your work as a pastor. A new sense of self will emerge through this work, and you will be able to function differently in your close relationships. Doing this work does not mean that you will live happily ever after. It only means that you will have more and better resources for addressing the inevitable life challenges that will arise in any case, and that you will be better connected with the people around you as you address these challenges.

In doing this work, you are breaking the patterns of generations of functioning in particular set ways. We are only the latest version of accumulated, unresolved emotional issues that we had little to do with creating but that, as members of that same emotional system, we have been perpetuating. Breaking the power of the generational patterns takes a tremendous act of courage and is truly heroic. People who do this work eventually (though not at first) become a kind of hero in their families and a resource for the following generations to create a new way of functioning emotionally in life. Working through the power of God's creative Holy Spirit, they are helping to bring new life and health to themselves and their people, so that their "days may be long in the land." If you are ready for this kind of adventure, then this book is for you.

PART ONE

A RESOURCE FOR MOVING TOWARD GREATER HEALTH

1

THE PASTOR'S OWN EMOTIONAL SYSTEM AND UNRESOLVED EMOTIONAL ATTACHMENT

WHAT IS UNRESOLVED EMOTIONAL ATTACHMENT?

Michael Kerr, in the book *Family Evaluation*, says: "The more anxious, frustrated, judgmental, angry, overly sympathetic, or omnipotent one feels about the problems of others, the more it says about unresolved problems in self." Have you ever had any of these feelings in relation to someone or to a group of people in your church? Omnipotence in this case means, "I know what your problem is and what you need to do about it." These are not unusual feelings, but we may not have thought that the feelings originated in our own families rather than with the particular parishioners involved. However, this explains why one person can be hugely upset with the behavior of someone while another person thinks, "It's no big deal."

David Freeman, in his book *Family Therapy with Couples*, says:

> Unfinished business is a present emotional reaction shaped by a past experience. It is a reactive response guided by strong emotional feelings based on past experiences of anxiety. Unfinished business does not allow for a thoughtful, creative response to a here and now situation; rather it triggers an emotionally reactive response to it. Whom we bring into our lives, our major life decisions, how we embrace important people, and the amount of closeness or distance we need emotionally are all shaped by the degree of unfinished business we carry into our adult lives.

Emotional attachment is a kind of symbiotic fusion in which the self of one person has not fully separated from another person's self. It usually involves dependency and a reaction to that dependency. Such statements as "I can't live without you" and "I don't need you" are both aspects of this fusion. One prominent aspect of emotional fusion is a confusion of who is responsible for what in terms of feelings and actions.

The more fusion that exists, the more difficulty there is in sorting out responsibility and, generally, the more blaming there is. The more fused we are, the more we believe the other person is somehow in charge of us.

All families—as well as all close relationships—have a certain amount of emotional fusion. It goes with the territory of human community. Unresolved attachment is the fused aspects of our lives that we carry with us from our family of origin into our adult lives. It has less to do with specific, perhaps traumatic events and more to do with the ongoing, daily patterns of emotional functioning we experienced within our families.

When we leave home we have emotional grooves, just like the old records, solidified within us. Here is a personal example. I was an only child who grew up with just my mother as a parent. It was inevitable that there would be a certain amount of emotional intensity between us, living together on our own, and we both managed this with a fair amount of emotional distance, which we were both more comfortable with. It was not an angry or hostile distance, and there was never any question of her love for me.

When I got married, living with my wife, Lois, was like a repeat of the situation with my mother. The only model I had for living with a woman was the way my mother and I had done it. Lois, quite naturally, wanted to be more emotionally involved with me than did my mother. I had no idea of how to do that, even though I agreed theoretically that it was a good thing. Lois was the emotional pursuer, and I was the distancer. This contributed to a pretty intense interactive process between us that is commonly called "marital conflict."

This is a simple example of how a past emotional pattern of adapting to the intensity of a relationship continues to affect and shape the present. I grew up and left home with the issue of how to develop and manage myself in a warm and open emotional closeness unfinished. We all enter adulthood with similar kinds of unresolved emotional patterns well established in our personalities.

ANXIETY, ATTACHMENT, AND REACTIVITY

Anxiety significantly affects each one of us. The story of Adam and Eve's disobedience, for example, introduces the issue of anxiety and distance. As soon as they ate of the forbidden tree, they hid from God's presence and covered their nakedness from the full view of the other. Anxiety is about a sense of vulnerability to some threat. In the story of Adam and Eve, the threat is in God's anger at their disobedience and in a sense of shame with each other about who they are and what they have done. Anxiety is a very uncomfortable experience, from which we want to distance ourselves. We deny who we are and what we have done in order to feel more comfortable. We do not want to be known. Reactivity helps us to hide from this vulnerability; we can put the focus elsewhere, on others rather than on ourselves. We blame and evade.

All of us hide parts of ourselves from others, and maybe even from ourselves. We each use the psychological defense mechanisms of denial, displacement, projection, and blame—all of which are attempts to avoid anxiety. Because of this hiding of self from others, our relationships with others are inevitably disturbed.

Our unresolved emotional attachment is most evident when we experience anxiety. Anxiety-producing situations normally trigger emotional reactions. The greater the anxiety, the more likely it is that these old emotional patterns will come into play. Here are two simple tests for the presence of unresolved emotional issues with one's family:

- How long does it take in a phone call or a visit home with either parent before you start sounding or looking or feeling or acting as you did at adolescence?
- To what extent can you talk with any family member about yourself or any other topic without becoming reactive to that person and his or her position, or to the person's reactions to your position, beliefs, values, feelings, and actions?

In earlier books, I have characterized standard types of emotional reactivity in close relationships as follows:

1. *Compliance*—covering up who you are and what you think, feel, and do to fit in with those around you; seeking their support and approval
2. *Rebelliousness*—telling others in various ways that they can't control you and "You can't make me..."
3. *Power struggles*—being equally as critical of others as they may be of you; shutting them up or getting them to back off; showing how they are wrong and how they should be more loving or more accepting; or, in other words, trying to change them just as much as they are trying to change you and getting them to conform to your wishes
4. *Distancing*—breaking off emotional or physical contact or both

DIFFERENTIATION AND GROWTH

The emotional maturity of differentiation of self allows us to get out of these reactive patterns. It is the antidote to anxiety. Self-defining moves, or "I positions," in family based on more rationally defined principles move us further out of the emotional fusion of sameness that is required by the togetherness force. We feel less threat and less inclination to distance and hide from others. We are more comfortable being who we are openly and behaving in a way consistent with our beliefs and principles.

We focus less on how others are, or how they want us to be, and more on how we want to be in relation to them. We can then let go of the old reactive patterns more often, and the number of threats we perceive decreases.

Differentiation assumes a confidence in God's invitation, given often and in many ways in the Bible, to "Fear not, for I am with you." It allows us to take the lonely, courageous stands we occasionally need to take in life. It is an act of faith that says we can survive our vulnerability and not fear it. We do not have to put our trust in some apparently strong but actually false god that cannot deliver true security. Differentiation involves the understanding that the suffering, and the near-death experiences, we may have as a result of standing by our beliefs and principles is the best way to "find" our lives, since we do not have to fear "losing" them. It is the way to a healthier life and better relationships.

THE INTENSITY OF EMOTIONAL SYSTEMS
AND UNRESOLVED ATTACHMENT

Some degree of unresolved emotional attachment with our family is always with us, just as sin is always with us. And like sin understood as a part of our human condition, this attachment will never be eradicated. But any headway we can make resolving the attachment will increase the quality of our lives significantly and improve our ability to work with and relate to others.

If we do not attend to our emotional attachment, and many people don't, life will stay much the same for us. We can change marital partners, change churches, move to totally different parts of the world, or change occupations as a way to change our lives, but these family issues will still be with us, running our lives. We will not change. Wherever we go, whoever we are with, whatever we do, our same anxiety-based emotional patterns will control how we function. The same issues with family, and the emotional system they are a part of, will continue to affect the quality of our lives, our level of emotional maturity, our level of functioning with others, and perhaps even the length of our lives.

Unresolved attachment is not the same as how we "feel" about our family, whether we feel it is "wonderful" or "awful," or whether we think we are a "close" family or a "distant" one. The issues do not result primarily from specific acts of commission, such as "Dad always beat us when we did something wrong," or acts of omission, such as "No one ever said 'I love you.'" These acts are the result of an emotional process that lies below those specific manifestations, a process that exists whether dad ever hit anyone or whether family members were good at expressing love.

I usually ask the people I work with, "Tell me about your family." People tend to present their families in idealized terms—for example,

"We are a wonderful family; we are so close and never disagree." Or they say something like "Oh, I don't think I want to talk about them. We were not a very good family; we fought all the time. I try to avoid thinking and talking about them as much as possible." These summary evaluations may be clues to experience in family, but they do not reveal much about the emotional process in the family and what part of it the people have carried into adult life.

It takes time to discover how much of our current feelings, thoughts, and behaviors is affected by the family emotional process. This would be one short definition of unresolved emotional attachment. People tend to think of peace/agree families as "wonderful" and of highly conflictual families as "awful." It is much more complicated than this: both can have significant elements of hiding and distancing.

The ways our fusion with family and lack of differentiation emerge become most visible in repetitive patterns of feeling, thinking, and acting or reacting, particularly during times of tension. How we emotionally insulate and isolate ourselves while in relationships with others so that we can keep our level of anxiety at bay will become obvious in these patterns of reactivity.

How much contact, and the nature of the contact, we have with all family members is one indicator to note. The more intense the fusion, the more we will be either emotionally overinvolved or underinvolved with family. The two types of involvement are not qualitatively different; rather, they are two sides of the same coin. Emotional fusion is most obvious in overinvolved patterns, but distance and cutoff are also symptoms of fusion.

If cutoff from one or more members of the family exists, particularly with any previous generation, then the issues within family are intensified. The more cutoff that is present, the more intensity there will be. The unresolved issues from the cutoff are displaced into new relationships, such as with the spouse or children, and this continues the cutoff through the generations. The intensity could be focused on the church or some particular aspect of church life, or on beliefs, moral behavior, or many other aspects of life and faith. Cutoff creates more intensity and sensitivity to emotional issues in the new relationships. It takes several generations of increasing intensity to produce the major cutoffs that can develop in some families in which siblings or parents and children never see or talk with one another and even refuse to recognize that the other exists.

Degree of openness about differences and degree of meaningful emotional contact with each family member are another indicator. People may have contact with most family members but use emotional distance and lack of openness about their differences as a way to keep the anxiety at bay and reach some level of emotional comfort in one another's presence. They may take part in ritualized holiday get-togethers, and yet family members will not get to know one another better. They will be hiding from one another.

DISTANCING AND PURSUING

The whole spectrum of closeness and distance with others, from simple situational emotional distance to severe permanent cutoff, indicates that there are unresolved emotional attachments that will affect the feelings, thinking, and behavior of the people in the system, even when they have "grown up" and moved away from the family. Some members of the family will go out in search of "closeness," looking for it, for example, in marriage, in relationships with their children, with colleagues at work, in social clubs, by joining with others in social causes, or in the church. Such arenas are nearly limitless. Depending on the intensity involved, these people may become emotional pursuers in relationships.

Others will be emotional distancers. They have an equally intense desire to remain more aloof and not get "too close." They need their space. They think of themselves as "independent," as not needing anyone. Their focus is that they don't want to be "controlled" or "smothered" by anyone. Both types of people are the product of a similar kind of emotional intensity and will have similar levels of differentiation of self. And the two types often end up in a relationship with each other, acting as counterbalancing forces.

Physical distance is a popular form of cutoff. I put three thousand miles between my mother and me for a ten-year period. It helped to cut back on the sense of intensity I felt with her. I would visit with her rarely, maybe once a year, if that much. Each time I left Los Angeles and went back east, I felt relief. I would do OK in her presence for a day or two, but then I would want to start to disappear, go visit friends, or just go places where she was not. Although my mother was a fine person (my friends wished she were their mother), I found interacting with her too intense. This is not uncommon.

Murray Bowen said, "Time and distance do not fool an emotional system." We carry that emotional system with us as we move around the country. I have had a seventy-year-old counselee have the same reaction to his ninety-five-year-old mother that he had when he was a teen. Once these emotional patterns are established, we carry them with us wherever we go. He played them out with his wife, with his children, and with other women. They got him in a lot of trouble.

Some people experience the intensity through physical symptoms. These help people keep some distance as they treat and attend to their symptoms. Some become emotionally reactive, have a fight, or experience some other form of upset. Or they get depressed. I would tend to focus on little things I disliked, such as the way my mother chewed her food. And I would get bored and zone out on TV. Some people get through a family visit by drinking a lot or through some sort of social acting out. I found out later that my mom had similar reactions when with her parents. And her dad, my grandfather, had them with his.

Physical distance or proximity is not really the issue. You can live on the other side of the world and have good emotional contact with family, or you can live in the same house and have poor emotional contact. The point is that by distancing or cutting off we carry with us the unresolved emotional attachments that really belong in our family. We take them to new relationships and hope to resolve them there, to have a different experience than we had at home. The intensity can get focused on being different from them or, in rare cases, being exactly like them. The more determined we are to make the new experience different from (or like) home, the more likely we are to fail. Failure to differentiate a unique self at home mostly means a continuing failure to differentiate no matter where we go and with whom.

If we can become aware of these patterns and recognize our part in the issues with family, if we can see how we are a part of that emotional system whether we want to be or not and whether we like it or not, then we will have made a first step toward addressing the patterns. For example, blaming our parents for our problems and unhappiness means we will probably be prone to blaming whomever else we hook up with in our adult life for our continuing unhappiness. Or, if we always thought of ourselves as "wrong" at home, then we are likely to find ourselves depressed and guilty in our new relationships as well.

THE IMPORTANCE OF ADDRESSING OUR
UNRESOLVED EMOTIONAL ATTACHMENT

Unresolved emotional attachment with family affects our work as pastors and congregational leaders in many ways. The anxiety and reactivity that go with it are not relegated only to our immediate family relationships. The patterns are passed from generation to generation. This offers an explanation of the emotional mechanism involved in how the sins of the fathers and mothers are visited on the sons and daughters, and so forth.

A prominent issue in the church today concerns those pastors who have sexually abused parishioners. The pastors I have worked with who have engaged in this behavior have clearly had unresolved issues with their families that they have played out sexually. Many were abused themselves as children. But whatever the experience, their issues stemmed directly from their family. These pastors were usually regarded as "wonderful," sensitive caretakers in their congregations. Their female victims, who had their own unresolved issues, responded to their caring overtures.

Pastors who have not addressed their own family issues get in trouble in their churches in many other ways as well. Many of them get locked into power struggles with their congregations, with particular members of their congregations, or with their judicatories. Almost always, they get fired. Some engage in clearly illegal activities and act out socially, and they may even go to jail.

But most of us do not identify with these more extreme examples of pastoral difficulties. It is not that we are different from these pastors; we just do not have the same degree of emotional intensity that they have. All of us exist on a continuum of emotional reactivity. Most male pastors have felt a temptation to become inappropriately involved with a church member. And most of us have become focused on particular personalities in the church whom we are tempted to single out as our "problem" members and label with negative language. Or we have gotten locked into battles with a church board or committee that we had trouble letting go of. We understand the feelings involved.

We may not be as driven by our unresolved attachment to act it out in such damaging ways, but there is a large variety of perhaps less dramatic ways in which we do act out our lack of differentiation and, as a result, fail to be the resource to our congregations and members that we could be. Because of this, in many ways we do not provide the leadership we could to the church and its mission.

The Michael Kerr quote at the start of this chapter describes some of the conscious feeling reactions we can have to church members and situations. You may identify with and experience these feelings and attitudes. But there are other, less conscious patterns we carry with us that can cause just as much trouble. For example, these blind spots can occur quite easily while we are in the role of helping or caring for others. When, as pastors, we begin to give advice, sympathize with one side in other people's arguments, get stuck in their stories and try to figure out "answers" for or with them, participate in triangles, become overinvolved with and overly supportive of them in their problems, or, conversely, try to distance and get out of the helping relationship, we are manifesting our lack of differentiation. Chapter 2 will explore a few of these patterns.

2

SOME COMMON DIFFICULTIES IN MINISTRY RELATED TO UNRESOLVED EMOTIONAL ATTACHMENT WITH FAMILY

One of the best clues to the influence of our unresolved emotional attachments on our church roles is our level of anxiety, which can be seen in our conscious feeling reactions to particular church members and the situations they are connected with or to a specific aspect of our pastoral work. But there are other, less noticeably reactive responses that we might think of as normal or perhaps even desirable. This chapter discusses six common examples of how pastors may act out their less conscious anxious patterns and express their unfinished issues in ministry.

INDIVIDUAL FOCUS RATHER THAN SYSTEMIC FOCUS

An individual focus is one of the most common inheritances nearly all of us receive from our families. Most parents operate with an individual model of functioning that says a child's problems reside in the child. They think: fix the child, and you fix the problem. If their child is misbehaving, they focus on disciplining or punishing the child until the behavior is "fixed." In some families, the treatment program is "loving and accepting" the child until the behavior is "fixed." Sometimes "the problem" is in a parent, and he or she needs to be "fixed." Or the problem is in ·
a relationship, and it needs to be "fixed."

As with families, people in churches tend to diagnose problems using an individual model of human functioning. Problems in churches typically develop in one of three areas, and sometimes in all three:
1. Impairment in the functioning of a key leader, perhaps the pastor; this problem can be physical, emotional, or social in nature, or some combination of these (alcoholism would involve all three of these).
2. Conflict between particular leaders or groups within the congregation or between the congregation and the judicatory.
3. A larger group focus on a particular person or on a smaller group in the church that is seen as "the problem" that needs to be fixed; this is the scapegoat phenomenon.

All of these problems, even though they seem to be centered on or "caused" by one or more specific people, are symptomatic expressions representative of larger systemic challenges in the congregation or in a person's family. Anxiety in the congregation can be organized around and focused on these problematic people or relationships. The thinking is that if only this person or this group or this relationship could be "fixed," then "we" would be OK. The other is "the problem." So a great deal of energy goes into analyzing, diagnosing, and labeling "the problem" and trying to get change to happen. Often this effort only seems to aggravate the problem. Or if the problem is fixed, then another problem emerges somewhere else. The anxiety has moved into a new person or relationship.

A basic belief in systems theory is that there is no such thing as an emotional problem in just one person. Symptomatic people exist within a larger emotional context, and their difficulties developed within that context. We are each just a slice of the pie; the problem exists in and is shared by the whole pie. Take a person in your church whom you may think of as uniquely peculiar or problematic. Put that person back in the context of the person's family of origin, and he or she would quickly begin to make sense to you. You would say, "Now I understand."

When members in the congregation come to us to discuss a problem, they will often have a problem-person focus or see a group of people as a problem. If we fail to see these "presenting problems" as a kind of metaphor for the members' own family emotional issues and instead buy into their problem focus, then we are lost. As we try to solve the problem with them, we will become a part of it. For both of us, as Jesus said, it will be as if there is a little speck of dust in the other person's eye, while we have a log in our own. We will miss our part in the difficulties.

A systemic focus does not deny individual responsibility. We are each responsible for our part in the larger problem. Other people do not "make" us do what we do. But it takes a higher level of emotional maturity to be able to step outside of the reciprocating, automatic emotional interactions of a family system and become a different, more emotionally autonomous person. Normally we are all just caught up in our family systems, in ways we often fail to recognize, and we develop our self within that context. We tend not to see any options for how to be. The more intense the system, the more this will be true—especially when we think, "I am nothing like them."

We have to hear "the problem" as a starting point for learning about the parishioners and their emotional context. Or, if we ourselves have the problem focus, we have an opportunity to learn more about ourselves and our own unresolved emotional issues. This is a powerful way to look at issues and people in the church. For example, our stewardship committee may seek to get particular people to donate more. This is a good way to create reactivity in these people and have the whole program blow up in our faces.

Having specific goals is good and desirable, but having them focused on specific problems "out there" or on changing other people could get us in trouble. How can we broaden our understanding of the problems (for example, around giving in the church) in a systemic way so we can see how everyone participates when some members underfunction around stewardship? The best goals have to do with the behavior of the person or the group setting them. The correct question is, What will they do or not do to achieve the goal? It is not, What will they get others to do? Might it be a stewardship goal that some people decide to give less? Think about it.

When we are tempted to look elsewhere for "the problem," we need to enlarge our understanding of the problem to include ourselves. How might we be helping to keep things stuck? What does the problem mean for self? How does it help to preserve a particular view or understanding of self? By focusing elsewhere, do we keep our own anxiety at bay or maintain a sense of personal safety? What are the feelings, losses, sadness, fears, or vulnerabilities that having a problem focus helps us to avoid? Can we more directly address the underlying anxiety in the system or in ourselves?

FOCUSING ON CONTENT RATHER THAN PROCESS

This is related to the first point. When we are focusing on the content of people's stories, as they tell us about their difficulties, we then start buying into their point of view and their anxieties. How we respond to their stories will determine how things will go. If we join in their focus on what others do, the discussion will not lead to change. If we can hear their stories as being about their own anxieties and how they try to maintain a sense of security or safety by having an other-focus, then we may be a resource to them in thinking through their issues.

Take Jane, for example. After her mother's death, Jane was trying to get her elderly father to leave his hometown, where he had lived all his life, and move 1,500 miles to be closer to her. He was resisting her efforts. As an adult she had always been somewhat critical of him, and now, with the death of his wife, she was even more anxious about how "poorly" he was managing things. When she went to her pastor with this story, the pastor helped her to see that maybe her father's "stubbornness" about moving was less the issue; rather, the issue was actually about moving closer to Jane. The pastor asked Jane to check this out with her father. Jane discovered that her father felt "criticized and pushed around" by her a lot. He just wanted to keep his distance from her so he could live his own life as he wanted to.

The goal of such pastoral conversations is to help people put their stories into a larger context that includes their own part in the emotional process of the story. Process is about *how* everyone participates in the difficulties and, then, what people can do about their own participation, which may lead to a different outcome. Process is about who does what, when, and how. People can easily focus on others, telling us what "others" do and maybe even "why" they do it, while leaving out their own part in the process, which is actually the only part they can change. Getting clear about self's part in the process is not always easy or self-evident. Once Jane understood that the issue was not "a stubborn father" but his distancing from her "pushiness," she was able to modify her part in the process by better managing her own anxiety, and eventually her father began to consider a move.

We achieve this goal by exploring the process through asking questions and being curious about how things work. It won't work to tell people "this is what is going on." It would be nice if things were that simple and we could get change just by telling people what is happening. People need to hear themselves talk and to put the process together for themselves. Our curiosity about how the process works is the best resource we can give them. It invites them to think more clearly about what is happening.

The pastor, as listener and helper, needs to be neutral about the issues of blame in a story, detached from the emotionality of the story, and curious about the process of interaction between the parishioner and those with whom he or she is having difficulty. The pastor should be most curious about the parishioner's thinking, feeling, and behavior that leads to his or her way of participating in the problem. This should then lead into the larger emotional background for the person, quite often in the family of origin.

If we have difficulty doing this, then our own unresolved attachments are taking over. It may be that the content of the parishioner's stories closely parallels some experience of our own or stirs similar anxieties. Jane's pastor could have had a father who died alone in another city and carried a feeling of guilt about this. So to avoid her continuing sense of guilt, the pastor may have shared the focus on Jane's father and his "stubbornness." We are protecting ourselves when we join with people in the content of their stories.

One pastor was counseling a single-parent mother (the divorced father had moved overseas and broken off contact) who was attempting to control her fifteen-year-old son in ways doomed to failure and destined to create further disruption. The pastor, who had no children of her own, was colluding with her parishioner in trying to figure out how to control the son through behavioral techniques. In talking with the pastor, I became curious about the pastor's anxieties. She deflected this focus and tried to convince me of the seriousness of what the boy was getting involved in and that something needed to be done. Eventually, we began discussing her family. It turned out that she had had a younger brother who had gotten into "a life of crime and drugs," and she had always felt badly that she hadn't been able to "save" him.

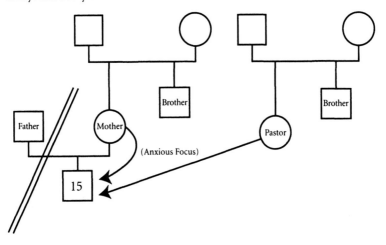

I asked her how much of her anxiety about this unresolved issue in her family was coming into this case. Her answer was "quite a bit." As it turned out, the parishioner mother also had a brother who had "gone bad," and she had feelings similar to her pastor's. Here were two unresolved family of origin emotional patterns getting focused on this boy. The anxious imaginations of the mother and the pastor were both acting out of these patterns, emotionally seeing a replay of an old drama and reviving old feelings of hurt, sadness, guilt, and loss.

The mother began to see her part in the process when the pastor could step back from her issues and become more neutral about the mother's story. The pastor was able to be more sensitive to the underlying fears and sense of failure in the mother and the son. The mother became less anxious, and things began to quiet down with her son. Of course, the pastor had some work to do with regard to her own family and her brother. This eventually became a liberating experience for her.

In this case the mother also worked at getting to know her brother better. She also asked this brother for his help in understanding her own son. She had always seen her brother as a "problem" rather than as a resource. This stance changed the basic dynamic between them, and, as a result, the brother took more of an interest in his nephew. This became a positive relationship for the boy, and the woman felt as if she had her brother back.

Here is another simple example. A fellow pastor generally did a good job of following people's thoughts and experiences when counseling them. He presented a situation to me in which he was talking with a committee chairperson about a conflict in which the chairperson was involved. On occasion this otherwise talkative parishioner would go quiet and periods of silence would ensue. I asked the pastor how he handled the silence. It turned out that, in essence, he would start thinking and talking for the chairperson, taking responsibility by proposing what might be happening. In response the chairperson seemed to become more confused.

I asked what was going on with the pastor in these silences. We eventually got to how his mother would go silent, lose focus, and stop functioning when she was upset about something. Quite naturally as a child, he then became anxious. As the oldest child, he overfunctioned with his mother and replaced his more emotionally distant father. When his anxiety kicked in around his mother's "shutdowns," he would get active and try to "get her back in gear." The same pattern took over in his work with the parishioner.

What we learn from such examples is that a content focus can happen in any part of our work as clergy, not just in counseling. Anxiety causes us to focus on the immediate content and keeps us from seeing the larger emotional process. The anxiety may often stem from unfinished issues from the past and the emotional process in our family of origin. Facing our own vulnerability to the unresolved fears, hurts, losses, and sadness that we have been trying to protect ourselves against will help us not to collude with the issues of those we talk with.

In one case, a church officer's strong homophobic reaction to any discussion of homosexuality in the church went back to his having a gay brother. This was a secret he kept from everyone until his pastor began to explore his family with him. He had totally cut ties with this brother and tried to avoid the unresolved emotional issues by vehemently arguing against any inclusion of "gay issues" on the agenda of board meetings.

THE PACING OF CHANGE
AND THE IMPATIENCE OF THE PASTOR

When a pastor needs to have people get better or have situations resolved quickly, it often means an issue of competence is involved. If the pastor tries to move things along, becoming impatient with the slowness of others, then this could well be an unresolved issue from family. If the pastor is trying harder to get a good outcome than the ones who are more directly involved in the problem, the pastor has become a part of the problem. The people involved then have to respond or react to the pastor's impatience rather than think more clearly about their issues. The experience becomes unsafe for them. They have difficulty being themselves and wandering around in their confusion because the pastor expects them to sort out the issues *now*. People need time to think things through for themselves, to discover their own voice, and to develop their own wisdom and strengths.

It is amazing how we can be aware of how long growth and change take in our own lives and yet expect other people to quickly "get" what needs to be done and do it. When I was training pastors in family systems work, this issue came up nearly every week. What often lay behind it was the pastors' need to feel competent and adequate. If their counselees would hurry up and get better, then the pastors could feel better about themselves too. It is the same for pastors who need to see change happen in the church "now."

Change requires some degree of feeling safe, of feeling OK with "the new" that will emerge in the change. If people don't change even when they can see a way to do it, it may be because it feels too "risky" for them. Safety is the issue to address in these situations. How can people feel "safe enough" while they experiment with changing self?

Often, "impatient" pastors have an overfunctioning role in family in which they think their job is to make things better or at least to calm things down for others. This confusion of responsibility for change, or who is responsible for what, is an issue in their own family. Then it gets repeated in the fusion with their church. When people balk and stall and resist, as may have happened in the pastors' own families, the pastors feel impatient and push harder.

When people are ready to change, they might respond to a slight nudge, an invitation, or a suggested direction from pastors. They respond because maybe it was their idea to begin with or because they were nearly ready to implement it and were feeling safer about the change. That is what allows them to risk being different.

When do people feel safe enough to move and tackle problems differently from how they have in the past? That is a critical question. I often ask impatient people I work with, "Could you just be present in your family and not expect anything to be different or anyone to change?" Then I quote the wise training maxim from *Alice in Wonderland*: "Don't just do something. Stand there!"

INCLUSION/EXCLUSION

Now here is a question you might never have thought of before: "Who is church for you?" The question parallels one I often ask people I work with: "Who is family for you?" It is always interesting who they include and exclude from their sense of family, in terms of who they do and don't actively relate to. Often I have pastors in supervision with me say they are doing counseling with "the whole family," and then I discover that the father has never attended or even been invited to a single counseling session. These pastors were working only with the children and the over-involved parent, who is nearly always the mother.

In family counseling, the mother is commonly the one who calls for help, brings the kids in, and defines the father as uninterested in the situation. Pastors often go along with the mother's limits and definitions of the problem. In my practice, when the wife or mother calls for therapy and I ask for the father or husband to come in as well, she often says he won't come. Ninety-nine percent of the time I have been able to get him to come in and to participate in the counseling. It is not that the mother is lying or really doesn't want him to come. He probably has said "no." It can be our anxiety about pushing the issue with the father that leads us to collude around this arrangement. The collusion results from our own unresolved issues in family, usually involving a distant father in our own home. To collude with the caller on this issue and exclude the father not only dishonors the father but increases the chances that the counseling will fail.

One pastor who said she was doing family counseling had not invited the father to attend. I insisted that she get him in, and she did. Then she showed me a videotape of the session, and I saw she had not physically included the father in the group. She practically turned her back to him and spent most of the time talking with the mom and kids. When she saw this on the tape, she got it. Almost immediately she began talking about how her own "emotionally distant father" had "never really been a part of the dealing with family difficulties." It was mostly she and her mom who tried to deal with things. She simply didn't know what to do with a father in her life or in her counseling. As she got into her own family of origin work, one focus became getting a relationship going with her father. Her picture of him as "emotionally distant" began to change significantly.

Apart from counseling situations, whom do you include or exclude when discussing difficulties in the church? Do you talk in depth with everyone who plays a part in the process, or do you get together with only the people whom you agree with, who are on your side, or whom you think you will get along with and won't feel too uncomfortable with? Are there church members you exclude because they are not "church" for you? Are there family members whom you don't think of as family for you?

It is more difficult to work on problems in a group if everyone involved in the problem is not involved in the discussion. What in your own unresolved attachments with family gets you to talk only with particular people and to ignore others? What is your anxiety about here? How might you be undermining change in the church by whom you include and exclude as church for you? How does this affect your work as a leader in the church?

INITIATING OR JOINING CONGREGATIONAL TRIANGLES

Murray Bowen once said, "Doing therapy is three-quarters staying out of triangles and one-quarter defining self." The same goes for our pastoral conversations. Triangles are a part of the human condition. They go with the territory. They are what we do when we avoid taking responsibility for our part in the process. In the Genesis story, God, Adam, and Eve are initially in what I call a triad: an open, direct, three-way, one-on-one relationship in which no one talks about the others behind their back. But the serpent introduces a triangle just by talking to Eve about God's "real intent," rather than its own intent in creating doubts about God. Many of our triangles focus on speculation about other people's motives.

Triangles are our most common way of avoiding closeness and connection with others. They are the way people stabilize their relationships by externalizing their anxiety onto someone or something else. Talking with one family member about another family member is a standard example. This occurs a lot in individual counseling and, for that matter, in everyday pastoral conversations. By talking about someone who is not present, we keep a comfortable distance from the person we are with, although it may resemble a kind of closeness and intimacy. Here is an example.

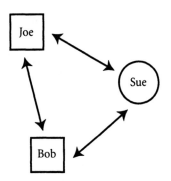

When Joe gets together with Sue and they talk about Bob, it looks as if Joe and Sue are close. But their closeness is only in their apparent agreement about Bob. They may not be in as much agreement as they appear to be. When Sue and Bob get together, they talk about Joe, acting as if they are the close twosome and Bob is the problem person. But then Joe and Bob might meet and begin talking about Sue and her problems. In none of the discussions do the people involved talk directly with each other about each other and say to their conversational partner what they have said about that partner to the third person. That would be a more open, direct, and possibly closer relationship.

One pastor told his secretary his private thoughts and opinions about the church treasurer that he had never verbalized to the treasurer. When the secretary spoke with the treasurer, she tried to "help" her boss by offering "helpful advice" to the treasurer. He immediately knew where this advice must have come from and began bad-mouthing the pastor with other board members for interfering with his work. The other members then began to take pro and con positions on the pastor's behavior, and before long an uproar was brewing that he knew nothing about.

The more anxiety we feel, the more likely it is that we will triangle. The pastor began this triangle by telling his opinions to his secretary. He was uneasy about dealing directly with the treasurer. The secretary had her own issues with the treasurer (which she was not open with him about), and this became an occasion to work at them, while believing she was only helping her boss. If we want to be a resource to others, it is essential that we avoid such behavior. We have to refocus the conversation back to the self of the person telling the stories about others. When anxious, we as pastors can join in our parishioner's anxiety and focus elsewhere with that person. This helps to maintain distance all around the system.

Triangles are so easy to form that we slip into them quite naturally. They function primarily to absorb anxiety in the system. While they do accomplish this in the short term, in the long term they become chronic and contribute to greater unease and difficulty in the system. In doing counseling, I had a maxim that said if things aren't moving with a counselee, think triangles. What are the triangles going on that I don't know about or am not paying attention to? Or, am I in a triangle in some unrecognized way?

In the church community we may triangle with others out of apparent concern for someone else or for some situation in the church. Whatever the motive, it is still triangulation. One pastor complained to me that he could not get a certain man to talk about himself. He would only talk about his wife or children. We looked at a videotape of a counseling session, and the pastor was amazed to see how his own questions and comments elicited this focus on others. He realized that he sensed the man's lack of ease in talking about himself and he colluded with this uneasiness; the pastor himself was also uneasy. Of course this went back to the pastor's own distant relationship with his father and how anxious he would be to ask such direct questions of his father.

There is a kind of general gossipy way of talking that focuses on others and what we have heard about them. This, in itself, is not always a problem and can sometimes help in letting us know about someone who, for example, may need pastoral attention. But it is too easy to maintain this style of relating in more difficult circumstances and problematic situations. People will often slip their triangular agendas into these conversations. Where does the particular member you are talking with fit in with the problem? What part of the problem does he or she carry or contribute to? What are the issues being avoided by focusing elsewhere? What is going on with you that causes you to collude with this?

This behavior is almost always about the way we function in our own family of origin. Many pastors seem to be closer to their mothers than to their fathers, and their pastoral conversations tend to replicate that early family triangle. One of the goals of family systems work is to be able to achieve a one-on-one relationship with every family member. This means you can sit with any family member and talk with him or her only about yourself, or the family member, or your relationship with each other without needing to focus on others.

When you are with your dad, do you tend to talk about your mom? Or a sibling? Or work? Or some sport or hobby or other typical male talk? Or when you are with your mom, do you do the same kind of thing? How often does real, one-on-one talking happen in your family? How often does it happen in your church relationships?

This type of conversation is not easy. I don't know anyone who does not find it difficult from time to time. Avoiding or not initiating triangles in the church goes against the grain of how we commonly operate. Often we may stumble into them and need to understand how to manage ourselves in them. Any progress in these attempts will have big payoffs for our church leadership and our ability to be a resource for our parishioners.

JOINING WITH THE PURSUER TO PURSUE THE DISTANCER

Joining with the pursuer to pursue the distancer is a common form of triangulation. Therapists do it in marital and family therapy all the time, and pastors join with the pursuers in their church. Such behavior involves accepting the myth that the pursuer wants closeness and is healthier and more prepared for intimacy than is the distancer, the one who appears to avoid closeness. Pursuers tend to be people who have read the self-help books and who can talk the talk of intimacy. They articulate the values that we tend to believe in and seem to be "our" kind of people. But these people may fail to recognize that people exist in reciprocal relationships and that we need one another to balance out these relationships. Pursuit is a good way to keep distance. There is a reason that pursuers end up in relationships with distancers. It helps with their uneasy issues around intimacy.

For example, when anxious, a particular wife tends to focus on her husband's "poor communication skills"—something his friends, his fellow workers, and his boss of many years have never considered a problem for him. In talking with this couple, their pastor kept her focus on the wife's anxiety and what she does with that rather than joining in a focus on the husband's "difficulty communicating." Then she turned to the husband and asked what he did when he experienced his wife's anxiety. They both had old underlying fears that led to their patterned behavior. They were able to explore their pursue-distance patterns and the experience of anxiety for both of them, talking about things they had never talked about, so that they found a way to get out of the patterns.

Closeness involves a vulnerability that we all find difficult. When we focus on the flaws and shortcomings of the distancer, we can ignore our own difficulties with intimacy and maintain a sense of safety for self. As pastors we tend to overvalue the pursuers in our church and undervalue the distancers. If we are pursuers ourselves, this can be a "double whammy" for certain people in the congregation. We will find that they keep even greater distance from us. In the previous example the wife tried to offer herself as a kind of "cotherapist" to the pastor for the distancing husband. If the pastor joined in and pursued the husband as well, they would never make contact. This is a major way we have for keeping things stuck.

I generally make a practice of pursuing the pursuers, preferably in the presence of the distancers. I keep my focus on the pursuers and do not get distracted by their efforts to focus elsewhere (usually on the distancers). Pursuers tend not to be comfortable with a focus on self. This is their unrecognized need to distance, to keep self safe. My job is to stay curious about their need to keep the distance. Being critical is one way pursuers can get the distancers to keep their distance. If the pastor or therapist joins with the pursuers, the distancers will distance right out of the relationship.

I had no problem keeping distancers involved in therapy and getting their participation. The pursuers were often amazed at how open the distancers would be with me and would say something like "How did you get him to talk so much? I have never heard him say things like that." The distancers would see me pursuing the pursuers with my interest in them, rather than joining in on a focus on the distancers. Then I listened to anything the distancers did say and invited them to expand on this only as they became ready and felt safe enough to do so.

Pastors who are addressing issues in their own family will be able to make congregational life safer for all members. That is the key. The main way to increase involvement and commitment in the church is for pastors to be a safe, less anxious presence. The same goes for the leadership of the church. People will respond to that.

Closeness and intimacy are a challenge for us all and are frequently misunderstood. What many people often mean by "closeness" is "sameness" in thinking, feeling, and behavior. Difference doesn't equate to closeness for them. The desire for unity based on sameness is a common congregational problem, but it just won't happen that way. Pushing for sameness causes distancers to distance more and develops more difficulties in the church.

The challenge is to recognize when we are being pursuers and are joining with the other pursuers in our church to help keep things the same. Being a pursuer, especially when dressed in Christian garb, is an excellent way to avoid the kind of connection with others that will make a difference. Remember, the serpent appeared to be concerned about helping Eve. The triangle was hidden behind the guise of helpfulness.

As you do your own family work, you will learn how to be with each church member in a less reactive and more interested, curious way. You will begin to hear members' stories about others as ways they try to take care of their own anxiety and vulnerabilities. You will be able to research their toxic or difficult issues as a neutral and, thus, safe presence. You will learn how to reposition yourself in triangles, define yourself with each church member, and establish a one-on-one relationship with each of them. To paraphrase Michael Kerr, you will learn how to be with church members and not let their problems get all over you. Instead, you will be a resource to members for their problems.

PART TWO

THE PASTOR'S OWN FAMILY

3

GETTING STARTED
ON DOING THE WORK

SELF AND THE SYSTEM: OUR EARLIEST TRAINING

The family we grew up in, our family of origin, is the most important emotional experience we have in life. Family colors our experience of the rest of our life, shaping the way we tend to perceive ourselves, our relationships, the kinds of decisions we make, and the ways we make them. While we may often experience family as our greatest source of stress, which leads us to want to distance from it, it can also be our greatest resource in creating change for ourselves and for enabling us to function maturely as adults.

As young adults, we each come out of our families with a story about them and about us—and about us in relation to them. Sometimes we tell our stories to others when the topic of parents or siblings or grandparents comes up. From a family systems theory perspective, these stories can be understood as justifications for our way of living, our beliefs, values, and the like. We may talk about these other family members as different from us and about how we do not want to live life the way they did. Or, sometimes, people use family as their reason for "why" they are the way they are: "With a family like that, who wouldn't be (feel, think, believe, act) the way I am? I could be different if they had been different. They made me the way I am."

It is easy to think of oneself as a victim in one's own family story. It is easy to ignore that we have made decisions about how we would be in our families. People have described their families to me and then said, in effect, "What do you expect from me with them as parents?" I might ask a female counselee in response to such a statement:

"What about your sister? Is she then also like you?"

"Well, no."

"So she dealt with her experience of the family in a different way from you. How do you account for the difference between you?"

"I don't know. We were just different."

"What kept you from doing it her way?"

"Oh, she has always been Miss Goody Two Shoes, and I decided as a young kid that . . ."

And now we are into her own decision making, something that she had at first denied in the victim framework.

When we tell negative stories about others in our family and how unchangeable they are, we do not realize that it is a way of keeping ourselves stuck. The labels we use to describe our family members can say as much about us as about them. Our labels for others reveal the position we have taken in life vis-à-vis those people. Labels also restrict our own ability to move in relationships, because they solidify a point of view. They keep us behaving toward others as if they are what we have labeled them.

If a man says of his wife, "She is so paranoid," I begin to wonder what he is not telling her. It is usually a lot. People with paranoid behavior normally have others around them who are withholding information and shading the truth. Paranoid people do not know exactly what information they are missing, but they have a sense that something does not fit. When other people become distant and noncommunicative, then they begin to fill in the gaps with their imagination. It is a circular or reciprocal process. Their paranoia and probable upset feelings become the justification for others not to tell the whole truth, which in turn feeds the paranoia.

If all we can see in other family members is that they are an "alcoholic" or a "liar" or "stingy" or "selfish," then our behavior toward them will be pretty well set in place. Our labels will limit our options. We will evaluate each encounter with them from that point of view, and usually the experience will just serve to build our case that "that" is the way they are. Each incident will only further prove our set idea of them, and we won't have any further curiosity about them. We won't learn anything about them with these labels in our head.

This is also where one of the resistances to doing family of origin work occurs. Developing a new view of family can be quite threatening. We sense that we may have to change the way we see family members, when we have built our personality and our view of the world on seeing things in a particular way. The whole idea of self, and our way of being in the world, has to change if we begin to change our view of family.

Family work requires that we stop seeing family members in simple terms as—for example—saints, sinners, clowns, vagabonds, or alcoholics. We need to see each of these people in a fuller and larger context. I came out of my family with a sense of shame about them. I never would have said this clearly until I first formally presented my family to others, but then I realized I had had this sense for a long time. My mother had been married four times, and I essentially grew up without a father. For a young boy in a small town, not having a father was embarrassing when I didn't know any other children without a father. I thought at the time that my grandfather was almost a bum, and he seemed to hang out with men like himself. Alcoholism was a major theme in the family. My family members just didn't seem like adequate people I could be proud of, and I never talked about them to friends.

Once I began family work, I realized this sense of shame was deep inside me. The shame was not only about them but about me. I had harbored a secret fear that I was going to "end up in the gutter," as I imagined my unknown father had, and that I was never going to "make it" in spite of my obvious accomplishments academically and professionally. This is part of the reason I kept my distance from family members. I didn't want my family to somehow "rub off" on me. So when I did my first "presentation" of my family to about twenty other professionals, I cried through a good bit of it. The tears were partly about this sense of shame of revealing who "we" are. I felt hugely vulnerable, almost naked in front of them.

However, as I did the family work, this sense of shame just seemed to melt away. As I got to know the members of my family better, I had a greater sense of what they had dealt with in their lives, of what they had managed to overcome given what they had been up against. Unexpectedly, I began to feel proud of them and what they had done. I had no idea this would happen. Interestingly, I also began to feel better about myself. My own unrealistic fears about myself began to melt away. I became much more comfortable with who I was.

This is how family can become one of our biggest personal resources, particularly in terms of our own self-image and self-esteem. What I had thought of originally as part of the source of my shame became my biggest resource in getting a more balanced picture not only of them but of myself as well.

WHO WILL PROFIT FROM DOING FAMILY OF ORIGIN WORK?

Most people will not have had my experience of family. Everyone's family is different, and the outcome of the work will be different. Rather than having an overly negative view of family, some people may have an overly idealized view of their family. Rounding out their view of family members and getting a more realistic sense of how the family actually functioned will often mean that they feel less oppressed in measuring up to the "giants" in the family.

For example, one woman's idealized image of her parents' marriage became a problem for her when she got married. She was surprised to find after marriage that she and her husband argued over their differences. She believed this meant something was wrong in their marriage, and she left him and moved back home. When she told her parents that she had left because of the arguments, her parents said, "But disagreements are a normal part of marriage." She said, "But you two never argued. Your marriage was good." They responded, "We argued all the time." She said, "No you didn't. I never once saw you argue." They said, "Well, we decided to never argue in front of you. We didn't want to upset you."

Many people say, "My family members have their problems, and I have my problems, but the two are not connected. I can make headway on my problems and let them do whatever they want about theirs. I don't have to get embroiled in theirs again." By putting distance between them and family, they manage to preserve this fantasy. But anytime they go back to be with family, this idea is challenged. Our reactivity to family is revealed, and our involvement in their issues, and theirs in ours, should be clear.

Even then, not everyone wants to do family of origin work, nor should they. Once we "get it"—once we understand that our personal difficulties could be connected with our experience in family—we have made the first step. However, having this insight and doing the work are two different things.

Family work can be done only when people are calmer and less anxious. People who are still highly reactive and emotionally intense are not good candidates for doing family of origin work. Their encounters with family would only be more disturbing and upsetting to them and everyone involved. These people would come away from those encounters thinking as negatively of their family as they did before.

Motivation is also a concern. Given the difficult emotional demands of the work, not everyone is up for it. That is fine. No one should feel guilty about not doing it. It has to make sense as something that you want to do, and nobody can decide that for you.

Many of my past counselees choose to terminate our work together without doing any family of origin work after the issues they originally presented improved. They had achieved all that they wanted and were happy with that. We would have a discussion about how they might proceed, but when they heard the words "going back to family," they said, "No thanks." They didn't see the need, or, more often, they didn't feel up to it. I would say, "Fine, I am always here."

Some of these people would have difficulties reemerge at another phase of the life cycle or at another transition point in their lives, and they would come in again for consultation. Often they would become involved in family work at that point. One person came back to see me after five years. He said, "I never forgot the questions you asked me about my family, and I didn't want to deal with them at the time. But the questions stayed with me, and now they are bugging me and I want to know what to do about it." Actually a number of clients came back with this sort of thinking.

One woman had not had any contact with her mother for over twenty years. She and her husband came in initially with major marital conflict, and we made slow progress on these issues. The husband had his own family story that we worked on as well. The wife lived in the same city as her mother. If she saw her mother on the street, she would cross over to the other side. It took her four years of counseling, with gradual improvement in the difficult marital issues, before she was willing to contact her mother; afterward, she said, "It's the best thing I have ever done." Even then, we moved slowly in her family work, but she did pursue it and had a suitable outcome.

Some of the most heroic work I witness is by women who have been sexually abused by their fathers. It may take years to get to the point (and, again, it is always their choice), but when they can feel safe enough within themselves to have contact with the father, they do it. This is not the whole point in having contact; however, when they can sit one-on-one in the same room with him and say in a nonargumentative way, in effect, "This is what you did to me, and this is the impact that you had on me," in doing that they say, "I've got my self back. I feel in charge of myself for the first time in many years." Again I emphasize, if this contact happens at all, it is always at their pace and sense of readiness. I would never push this.

It does not matter what the father says in response, whether he admits what he has done or even remembers doing it. The woman is not looking for something from him. If he can admit what he did and even (rarely) ask forgiveness, that is fine, but it is not the point. Whereas many abused women pick abusive men for their partners, the women who have done this family work do the best job in picking more competent and caring men as partners. They can maintain their own sense of self within the relationship and have more satisfying sexual relationships.

I have never worked with a person who failed to profit from doing family of origin work. While everyone does it in their own way and at their own pace, their lives have always improved. In each case they have a new sense of themselves as well as of their families. I would never recommend the work if, in any way, people would not be physically safe. It is not appropriate to do the work if they cannot first get to a less reactive and more objective place in their lives. These are some of the prerequisites that I will discuss in chapter 7, which focuses on readiness to do the work.

FINDING A COACH

You can do this work on your own without the aid of a coach, but it will be much more of a challenge, and it will likely go more slowly because of things you will miss. A coach usually brings greater objectivity and more familiarity with the theory. It can help to bounce your own thinking off another, knowledgeable person.

Not every community has a counselor or a person who is well acquainted with Bowen family systems theory. Lots of people do "family therapy," but you need to interview them to see if they do family of origin work from a Bowen perspective. At a minimum, whatever their theoretical orientation, if they say they do family of origin work, they need to be respectful of all members of the family, neutral around family emotional processes (that is, not take sides), see multigenerational work as a resource to the individual and, most important, have done their own family work.

The Bowen Center may be able to help you find a coach (see the appendix). They have a mailing list of all of the people who have done training with them. They may not be able to "recommend" coaches, but they may be able to give you some clues to follow. Also, they run courses for distance learners, who come to Georgetown four times a year for three days, and have phone supervision in between these visits. These courses are open to people of all professions, not just therapists, and the supervision is focused on whatever practice orientation a person has. Many clergy have been in their program.

Also, a program started by the Rev. Larry Matthews, called "Leadership in Ministry," which is just for clergy, does something similar. Matthews has sessions twice a year in various parts of the United States. Other training centers around North America may also be helpful. A number of seminaries are conducting ongoing training in family systems theory in their continuing education departments. Check the Internet and call around.

4

THE AUTHOR'S OWN FAMILY

THE GOALS OF A FAMILY PRESENTATION

In any training group I run, I always present something of my own family of origin work for the group as a way to start. It is my way of trying to make it a safer experience for people by showing that I'm not asking them to do something I wouldn't do. It also models some of the basic elements of a presentation. I am a long way from that first time I presented my family, when I was shaking and crying, but I still feel vulnerable at times. I would like to do the same thing in this chapter as I do in my training.

A family of origin presentation has three main goals. The first goal is to help us, as presenters, to think through the issues in our family from a Bowen theory perspective. If you have ever drawn your own family diagram, you know that the act itself is helpful. It may be one of the first steps in getting more emotional distance from your family. It requires that you start seeing all family members in a larger, multigenerational perspective, not just in relation to you. Then, as you start to fill in dates, clarify relationships, connect important events, and find the blank areas that you know nothing about, it begins to stimulate your curiosity. Most people's first presentation to a group is full of gaps and holes and question marks. It is fine that information is missing. That is where we are starting.

When presenting whatever we do know about our families, we are also thinking about how they and we functioned. As we begin to learn about Murray Bowen's concepts and apply them to our family, we can begin to make better sense of our family and our place in it. This is a process that may take years and perhaps many presentations. Each time, we learn something more. Each time we talk about particular people and relationships, we come to see them in a new light. Even now, after many, many presentations, I learn new things, develop questions I would like to ask, and think of things I would like to address.

The second goal involves the role of the group. Group members are not simply passive listeners in this process; rather, their role is to help the presenters think further about their family issues. A typical presentation runs for one and one-half to two hours depending mostly on the time available to the group and how the group is structured. Presenters normally get forty-five minutes to an hour of uninterrupted time to talk about their family. Then the group asks questions that are designed to help presenters think further about their family. Group members do not, and should not, offer interpretations of family processes to the presenter or say things like, "Don't you see how . . ."

While listening to a presentation, group members can form questions that may open up new areas of exploration for the presenter. These questions serve as practice for using the theory to become family researchers rather than family interpreters. The best questions stimulate curiosity about our family processes; they don't elicit defensiveness. If they do the latter, they probably have an interpretative element in them. Listening to a presentation also helps to develop neutrality around family processes. It is easy to believe that we have some great insight about a person's family and want to give them our interpretation, which almost always comes out of our own family issues. As we listen to other people talk about their family, perhaps similar to ours, we may achieve more emotional distance with ours.

The third goal is to determine where the presenters head next in their family work. "What would you like to do now?" is a typical start to this part of the presentation. Then, for example, "What would it be like for you to make contact with that cutoff aunt?" Or, "How do you think you might like to approach dealing with that triangle?" Or, "How can you find out more about the history of that relationship?" Or, "Who would be your best resource for learning more about that event?" Or (to an older sibling), "How could your younger sister be a resource to you?" Ideally, the presenter comes out of the experience with one or more directions to follow.

It is useful to tape presentations, preferably on video, for the presenter to review afterward. It is best to wait a week or two, or even a month, before viewing the tape. Often, presenters don't hear the questions that are asked at the time they're asked. They are so anxious or so set in seeing things a particular way that they miss the new territory a question opens up. Looking at the tape later, they may realize, "I didn't even hear that question."

Of course, absolute confidentiality must be agreed upon at the start. No one is to talk about anyone else's family outside of the group without that person's permission. The group cannot function if this happens. I remember making a presentation many years ago to a training group that included one of the board members of my agency. A couple of days later, I ran into another board member on the street and his first words to me were, "Hi, Ron. I hear you have quite a family." It didn't take me long to contact the other board member and address the breech of confidentiality.

Another rule is that presenters decide what they will and will not talk about. They don't have to "tell everything" if they don't want to. Whatever information they share is up to them. Group members are free to ask any question about any area they want to, and presenters are free to answer or address only what they want to. No one should feel compelled to "tell all" in their presentations. You can be sure that my presentation here is not "telling all."

MY FAMILY

Here is a simplified version of my family diagram for three generations. To keep things brief, I have left many people out and focus mostly on the relationship with my mother and her family, addressing a few of the sibling issues and the triangles in that extended family. Everyone in this diagram is dead now except me. By the way, in these presentations, we don't talk about our nuclear family, although you can put them on the diagram if you choose.

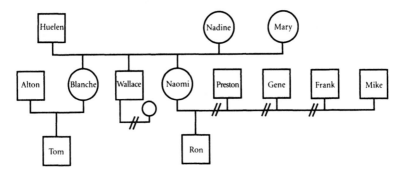

I was born in 1939 to my mother, Naomi, and my father, Preston. Naomi left Preston when I was eight months old. We lived first in Columbia, Missouri. At that time Columbia was a small college town of eighteen thousand people and home to the University of Missouri. My mother and I moved five times while I was in elementary school there. Some of those moves involved living with my grandparents (Huelen and Mary) because my mother had trouble paying the bills. We moved to Hollywood, California, in 1950, and while I was in junior high and high school there, we moved another six times. I lived at home while attending UCLA and then moved out for good when I went back east to attend Princeton Seminary.

In Princeton, New Jersey, during my last year of seminary, I met my wife, Lois, who was working at Educational Testing Service there.

I saw my father, Preston, only once—when I was ten—after Mom divorced him. I remember nothing of that visit with him. Naomi married again, for six months, when I was two. She left Gene because she did not "love" him. She said she had married him for the security of his money rather than for love but decided that didn't work for her. Her third marriage, also for six months, happened when I was in tenth grade. I suspected that Frank was gay (based on Frank's behavior toward me) but didn't tell my mother this. She soon discovered that he was gay, and the marriage was annulled. She had several boyfriends between each divorce and remarriage. Her fourth marriage happened after I had left home, and it lasted the longest, until Mike's death in 1987. Naomi died in 1989 of a rare lung disease at age seventy-four.

All four of these men had significant problems with alcohol. Naomi described them as "perfect gentlemen" when they were sober, but they turned mean and argumentative when drunk. Only Frank was physically abusive of her, and, at that point, I was old enough to fight him physically and essentially chase him out of the house. My mother had a restraining order put on him. It was a very tense time in both of our lives.

When Naomi left Preston, she got her first job the next day, at the University of Missouri, as a typist. She worked her way up to be the head of the typing pool and then eventually became the secretary to the vice president of the University. She worked for most of the rest of her life as an executive secretary.

Naomi never asked any of the men she divorced for alimony. She later explained to me that she didn't want to have that connection to them or be dependent on them. She left Preston because of his infidelity, not his drinking. When she left him, he said, "Well, don't you be asking anything of me." She said, "I won't, and don't you ask anything of me." He said, "What could I possibly want from you?" She said, "You'll see." By this she meant that he would not be able to see me. She explained later, after I began this work, that she didn't want his ways and values to rub off on me. The reason I saw him when I was ten was because she thought I was old enough to handle it. We didn't talk about any of this at the time.

I literally did not have a single conversation with my mom about Preston or ask about the history of their relationship until I began doing this work. I had suspected as a child, because of my mom's silence on the subject, that I was born out of wedlock, and I didn't want to talk to her about this if it were true. It was too embarrassing. I had heard once from my aunt that Preston was a drinker and lost jobs because of this, and I concluded that they'd had a brief affair and that now he was probably a drunk on skid row. This felt like one more source of shame among many in my family, and I just didn't want to know. When people asked me about my father, I said, "I don't have a father." I was the only kid I knew, until high school, who didn't "have a father." That is how I thought about it.

One of the first things I did when I began my family work was to write a letter to my mother to ask her about her relationship with Preston and what happened there. I was very anxious about this. I felt as if I were breaking a huge taboo, mentioning the unmentionable. I expected an atomic explosion in Los Angeles when she got the letter.

What I got back was a three-page, single-spaced letter giving the history of their relationship. The letter had the feel of her saying to herself, "Whew, at last he asked!" I was surprised to learn that they had been married for five years before I was born. They had led an active social life, but when I was born, my mother decided it was time to get serious. She said Preston didn't see the need. Along with the letter she sent a packet of letters that she had been saving all those years. They were letters to me from Preston, which, once I saw them, I vaguely remembered. They were simple attempts to be a father to me from the distance of Florida, where he had moved. When I met him at ten, he complained to mother, "My son doesn't know me." She said, "He doesn't know anything bad about you." She did not know what I had imagined about him. We never heard from him again after that visit.

The lack of discussion about my mom's marriage to Preston and most other serious topics, such as Frank's sexual orientation, was typical of how we managed our relationship—with a great deal of distance. Regarding Preston, she said to herself, "Ron will ask when he wants to know." I said to myself, "She'll tell me when she wants me to know." We conducted most of our life together with those two philosophies.

Mom very rarely asked me questions about my daily life. I was one of the first "latchkey kids," and I was free to do what I wanted after school. She never asked me when she got home from work what I had done that day in school, what I had done after school, with whom, and so forth. I knew that she loved me and in some ways doted on me, and that she was supportive, but she didn't like "to pry."

The first two years of my family work, all I did was ask questions of my family members. This felt like a big deal to me in a family that didn't ask many questions. My aunt Blanche said to my mom early on in the process, "Ron sure is asking a lot of questions." Mom agreed. But they got over their uneasiness with it because I did not appear to be building some kind of case against the family. None of my questions appeared to elicit any defensiveness from them. Plus, I made a point of never asking questions about myself, or how they saw me, or their relationship to me, or my development, or anything like that. It was all about them, the earliest members of the family they could remember, those early relationships, and their own family experience growing up. When they asked why I was asking, I just said that all these years I had lived in ignorance about my family and that I decided I wanted "to know more about who we are." If Lois and I had had children, I would have also said that I wanted to be able to pass on our family history to them. I think they liked that I wanted to know.

One time I took Mom and her sister (my aunt) Blanche to the little four-corners farming community in which they grew up, outside of Columbia. They enjoyed looking around. The houses they had lived in were still standing. This visit evoked a lot of family stories from them. We went to the country church they had attended and looked around the graveyard, where many family members of previous generations—including their mother—were buried. We talked about all the family members and other people buried there and what they remembered about them.

At one point Mom had wandered off on her own, and I saw her standing in front of a gravestone crying. I went over and put my arm around her and asked her what was happening. She said she had always wondered where her name came from. Her mother had died when she was three months old, and she had never asked her father. She was standing in front of the gravestone of her mother's best friend, who was also named Naomi. I can still get teary, even now as I write, about what a powerful gift that was for my mother from her own mother, whose picture she kept beside her bed everywhere she lived until the day she died.

We were talking another time, and, as I was asking questions, Mom started crying. I asked why. She said, "I so wish I could have done this with my father." I thought this was a powerful statement about how safe she was beginning to feel with me and with the overall process. She was finding it to be a valuable experience also. Once I asked with some trepidation, thinking she wouldn't know what to say, how she accounted for her four marriages. She quickly came back with, "I was looking for the love I didn't get from my father." After that we could talk about that relationship more, and I got to know more about my grandfather. We were breaking new ground.

When the time came to be more focused on the relationship between Mother and me, I jumped right in. I want to emphasize that it took two years of asking about her in her family before I did this. I had always had difficulty believing that anyone could be interested in me. If someone asked me questions about me, I wondered what they were up to and didn't say much. So I said to her one day, in a neutral tone of voice,

"Mom, I know you have always loved me. But I have always wondered if you were interested in me." She said, "Why would you say a thing like that? I have always been interested in you." Then I said, "Because you never asked me any questions." If I would have said this to her before the work of the previous two years, my voice would have been different, she probably would have cried, feeling accused and misunderstood, and I would have shut up. That would have been the end of that.

Instead, she said, "Oh, let me tell you what that is about." She then proceeded to tell me more about her relationship with her stepmother. After her biological mother died of pneumonia, brought on partly by Mom's birth, her father, Huelen, did not remarry until she was three years old. Huelen had loved his first wife deeply, as did both of Mom's older siblings, Blanche and Wallace. He married his second wife, Mary, so that his children could have a mother. Mom's siblings never accepted Mary and kept their distance. She quickly became the "wicked step-mother" for them. But she became "Mother" for Naomi, and Mary jealously guarded that relationship. She wouldn't even let Huelen get close to Naomi. Mary kept Naomi on a close tether; when Naomi got home from being out someplace, Mary peppered her with questions about who she was with, what she did, what next, and so forth. Mom said to herself, "When I have kids, I will never do that to them."

This put a whole new perspective on the issue for me. I moved from being somewhat resentful of Mom's lack of curiosity about me to seeing what it must have taken for her to hold back and not do with me as her mother had done. This was an act of love on her part rather than an act of disinterest. She wouldn't have known that treating me the way she wanted to be treated as a kid wasn't the best way to parent, that our situations were different. This is one way the multigenerational transmission process of anxiety works. To her dying day, Mom could not break this rule she had set for herself. She would say to me, "I know I am supposed to ask you questions, but I just can't." I said that was fine. I had decided that if I wanted Mom to know something about me, I would tell her and not wait to be asked. That worked pretty well for both of us.

This is an example of moving toward a one-on-one relationship, being able to talk about anything in the relationship between two people. But it was really slow coming for me. Perhaps we both needed some time to get there, but I think Mom was ahead of me. I say that "I jumped right in," but actually I had one false start. I was coming to Los Angeles for a conference, and I said I would like to spend a full day with her, maybe take a drive down to Laguna Beach and just talk. We had the day together, took the drive, but I hardly said anything of note. I was just trying to get my courage up to have a different kind of experience with my mother. Finally, near the end of the day, as we were heading back to her house, she said, "I thought you wanted to talk with me about some things." I said, "Right." We pulled in to a place to have some coffee, and I spent an hour asking her questions about her experience of being the single mother of a young child ("What was it like for you . . . ?" type of questions) and a parent with her own parents so close by. That was as good as I could do then, but it was a start.

Blanche, Mom's older sister, was the caretaker in the family. Part of Mom's reason for moving to Los Angeles from Missouri was to distance from this bossy older sister. Another reason, she told me later, was that she had run out of single men in Columbia. The move put more emotional distance between her and Blanche, and they saw little of each other after the move. With my family work they had reconnected and were doing pretty well together. They started having weekly phone conversations along with more regular visits until Mom died. This reconnection between other family members is a common outcome of the work.

When my mother was close to death, I called Blanche and said she had better fly out to Los Angeles. The next day she was there. At this point Mom was seventy-four and Blanche was eighty-three. Mom had stopped eating. The hospital staff and I had accepted this as her way of bringing an end to her incurable lung difficulties. She was weak and in a slight medication fog but was still aware and communicative. I picked Blanche up at the airport and took her straight to the hospital. She went into the hospital room, and this older sister saw the uneaten tray of food in front of mother. The very first thing she said was, "Sister, you're not eating your food." She proceeded to try to feed Mom. Mom, as the younger sister, compliantly took one bite but then refused anymore. Blanche said, "You're just as stubborn as you always were." Mother quickly replied, "And you are just as bossy as you always were." I got a kick out of that and laughed. Mom dozed off at that point, still distancing from her older sister. Those were about their last words to each other.

When Blanche married Alton, his mother moved in with them shortly after his father died. She died many years later, still living in their house, while experiencing a long period of Alzheimer's disease. They never hospitalized her. After her death my uncle Wallace moved in with them until he died of an overdose of alcohol and pills. After his death my grandfather moved in with them until he died. Shortly after his death, when it looked as if they were going to be free to travel and have an easier life, Alton developed a stroke condition that caused "brownouts," and he had to be closely monitored. Then he developed Alzheimer's disease. He had always been a tough, demanding, somewhat quick to anger man, and now he began to threaten violence. Blanche and Alton's son, Tom, who was living at home through all of these events, frequently had to step in to hold back his father. They eventually put him in a nursing home, where he died. Then Tom developed various ailments due to his drinking. Blanche, now in pretty bad shape herself, could no longer manage him, and he did as he wanted in the house. It was never clear to me who, at this point, was looking after whom. Tom was hospitalized and went sober many times, but it never lasted. When he died at age forty-seven, after Blanche had looked after so many people, there was no one to look after her. I was the only one, and I did it until she died in a nursing home with an organic brain disease.

Apart from the issue of rarely talking about anything of significance with me, Mom was like a typical youngest sibling in her parenting style. She was liberal, permissive, and easygoing. Her own family experience helped to strengthen this inclination. She had few rules, but she could discipline if it were needed, which it rarely was. I knew what the limits were and did not want to upset her.

My growing up was significantly different from that of my cousin Tom, who was also an only child. His parents were an oldest sister, Blanche, and an only child, Alton, both of whom were very strict and expected a lot of him. They focused much of their life around raising him, and, as he developed various behavioral difficulties growing up, they were superinvolved in trying to "straighten him out." But he never really got himself launched in life. He was a wild kid in his teens and young adult years. He did not seem able (though I am sure he was) to hold down a full-time job, and he never married.

On one of my visits to their home in St. Louis, Tom picked me up at the airport. Mom had already flown in from Los Angeles and was in the backseat. Driving back to the house, he pointed out a school building and said, "That is where I was first allowed to stay out past midnight." I knew this was an issue and said, "How old were you at that time, Tom?" He said he was nineteen. This was unimaginable to me, and I turned back to Mom and said, "I don't ever remember us having a discussion about what time I should be in by." She said, "That's right. Because you were always in before me." Tom gave out some kind of an exclamation that showed he got just how differently these two sisters had raised us.

I once presented my family to Michael Kerr, who commented on how "lucky" I was. He was referring to the fact that Mom had been trying to work out her unresolved issues with the men in her life rather than with me. She did not need me to be a certain way for her to feel OK. I was allowed to be a free spirit, to develop more or less as I wished and make my own decisions about my life. Life was very different for Tom.

My mother never once expressed hopes or expectations about what I would do when I grew up. She saw that as my job, not hers. She was surprised, however, when, without consulting her, I decided to go to college and was even more surprised when I decided to go to seminary and become a pastor. In fact, she admitted to me later, she was a bit ashamed of this decision and didn't tell her friends right away. She thought the church was full of hypocrites and that I was going to be one of them. Finally, she adapted to the idea and began to tell her friends. After they would say, "What?" she would say, "Well, environment tells." She had a wonderful dry humor that it took me a while to appreciate. Upon reflection, I don't think she was far off base.

One example of her humor occurred when I turned twenty-one. I was still living at home, getting free room and board but ready to head back east to seminary. Her birthday present to me was a piggy bank, with some cloth strips tied around it. I pulled them off and broke open the bank. Inside were twenty-one new $100 bills. She had never me given anything like this (she couldn't afford it), so I knew it was a big deal. She had been saving for many years to be able to do this. After counting the money I picked up the cloth strips and said, "But what are these?" She said, "They are apron strings." Most people would get this, but I didn't. Holding one in each hand, I said, "Apron strings. What would I want with apron strings?" She said, "Think about it." Then I got it. She was cutting me loose. An anxious feeling washed over me. I had been launched out on my own. While it was a scary feeling at the time, I eventually saw the wisdom and the gift in this. She wanted to get on with her life and didn't want to keep supporting me. I thank God that she was not a "child-focused" parent. She had her own life to live. Parents need to differentiate from their children as well as the children from the parents. In fact, successful parenting requires this.

By contrast, all of this was quite different for my cousin Tom. He was a perfect example of the family projection process at work. His mother and father had so many of their hopes pinned on him that, I think, it just piled up on him. Much of their anxiety was focused on him. They almost lived for him to accomplish great things in life, and the more he failed the more they worried and focused on him. He inherited their anxiety, and he treated it with alcohol. And as much as he appeared to resent their involvement in his life, he didn't seem to be able to live without it.

Tom was born relatively late in his parent's marriage, and he was very much wanted. They had had difficulty conceiving a child. So I was in the family long before him (even though they were older than my mother), and my aunt Blanche had become quite attached to me. I found her overwhelming and always felt as if I wanted to push her away. She was a very involved Methodist churchgoer, and her attachment to me grew even stronger when I became a pastor. Tom and I would roughhouse the relatively few times we were together as kids, and I vaguely knew he kind of looked up to me. It took a long time into the family work before I realized that I was more like an older brother for him within his family, even though many miles, with only rare visits, separated us. He admired my athletic involvements and tried to imitate them. His mother admired my faith involvement and held me up to him, but he didn't want to emulate that. I got talked about a lot in that family, though I had no idea of this. He was just a cousin to me. I didn't know this triangle existed.

So when I started this work, I couldn't get close to him. He kept his distance and was hesitant to spend time with me alone. At one point he had broken off an engagement to a "wealthy young heiress" who taught in the private school where he was the rugby coach. He wasn't saying why he broke it off to his parents, who had been quite excited about the engagement. On one visit to the family they asked me to find out why. I suggested to Tom that we go to a Cardinals baseball game, and he agreed happily. When there I said to him, "You know, I have been asked by your parents to find out why you broke off your engagement. But it is up to you whether you say anything. I don't need to have you explain it." He said he wasn't talking about it. And that was it. I said, "Fine."

After a couple of years I was on another family visit. At this point I had begun to realize my role as "older brother" for him and that this was part of his distancing from me. I was also aware of the triangle of his parents and me, with him in the outside position. However, an event happened that allowed me to shift my position in the triangle. We were all going out to dinner, and I came downstairs wearing a coat and tie. He made fun of the way I tied my tie and laughed at me. I saw a chance here and said, "You know, Tom, I never had a father to teach me how to do things like that. Some people here [looking at his parents] don't even notice if I am out of style. Would you teach me how to do it correctly?" He launched into it with gusto and was very caring in the process.

At the end of that trip he took me to the airport. We were there early and went to get some coffee. He said, "You know, you have been asking a bunch of questions, like why I broke off my engagement. Do you still want to know?" I said "Sure," and he began to open up, talking to me about his life. He had begun to feel safe with me. With my taking the one-down position about the tie, he felt more equal. He had remembered my questions. After this he began to take the initiative in contacting me. He came out to Los Angeles for my mother's funeral. He was gratified that, when he neared death, I assured him I would look after his mother. None of this could have happened without the family work.

Another family triangle took me a while to discover. I had always known that my uncle Wallace had died of an overdose of alcohol and sleeping pills. I can remember lots of family incidents around him and his drinking when I was a young kid. My grandfather was highly involved in trying to sober him up. In response to my questions, my mother and my aunt would begin to talk about his depression and even that his death was a suicide. But when I asked what he was depressed about, they shut up. They said, "He was just depressed." I tried several times to pursue this and finally gave up. I hit a similar brick wall when I asked about what happened to his marriage.

Several years later I was again trying to talk with Mom about Wallace's marriage. She said, "You know you used to ask about Wallace's depression? Well, here is the story." Columbia was a border town during the Civil War, but it was more on the southern side. Racism was prevalent, and blacks and whites lived in mostly separate worlds. Wallace was working as a chef in the big hotel in town. However his co-chef was a black man. One day it came out that Wallace's wife was having an affair with the black chef. When this became known, the "town fathers" came marching into the hotel kitchen and said to the chef, "Get your black ass out of town, and don't ever come back." He left town—and Wallace's wife went with him. Wallace felt he couldn't live down the shame of this loss, and he never recovered. He treated the pain with alcohol. Surely there was more to his depression than this, but this was a major turning point for him.

I wondered why it had taken so long for me to hear this story. Then I got it. I had been an urban, inner-city pastor very involved in racial issues, working with black people in the cities. During visits home I had expressed some of my views, and others had been imputed to me. I was in a triangle I didn't even know existed. Mom was uncertain about how I might take this story and was worried that I might ask her what she thought or did about this issue at the time. She just didn't want to deal with it with me. So it took her that long to feel safe enough with me to tell this story.

CONCLUSION

This is an example of some of one person's work. It includes some of the work I did over several years. A presentation earlier in the process would have spent more time in the generations above, beginning to look at how each line of the family developed and functioned in terms of the theory. It may not have had any "work" included because, to that point, nothing had been done. Everyone's story is different, and the work is different, so this is not *the* way to do it. The differentiating moves I made were not hugely challenging, partly because of the mother I had. More remained to be done, but—unfortunately for both of us—my mother's death came earlier than we expected. Since we knew she was terminally ill, and knew about how long she had left to live, the last year of her life was an amazing process for the two of us.

I could tell many more stories about the work and its benefits. I felt as if I grew up emotionally in doing it and resolved several personal issues—not all of them, as my wife can testify, but it was a great start toward being a more emotionally mature person. Lois would agree that I am definitely more available emotionally as a result of this work. The biggest immediate gift was what I gained by getting to know family members better and learning to admire their lives. The shame I had felt previously was replaced with pride of family, and this brought with it a similar shift in my own sense of myself. The inner shame that I felt for no clear reason melted away. When my family members died, I was able to be there wholeheartedly. If I hadn't done the work, I don't know how I would have managed the deaths.

5

THE BASIC GOAL OF THE WORK: DIFFERENTIATION OF SELF

DEFINING DIFFERENTIATION OF SELF

Within the Bowen theory framework, the basic goal of family counseling generally, and of family of origin work specifically, is to promote the greater differentiation of self within the family emotional system. Differentiation is a relative matter. No one is ever fully differentiated. Bowen posited a theoretical scale of levels of differentiation that went from zero to one hundred, with one hundred being the most differentiated possible. Both ends of the scale are hypothetical, and I doubt that anyone exists above the level of seventy-five or eighty. I have known two people who I think might have a basic level of about fifty-five or sixty. I think of my own basic level of differentiation as somewhere in the higher thirties, though I often can function significantly above that. Our functional level can fluctuate above and below our basic level of differentiation, which makes the basic level difficult to determine.

How do we define differentiation of self? The term comes from biology; cells develop from an amorphous, undifferentiated conglomerate into highly differentiated cells with specific functions or identities within the larger organism, but the cells remain connected to one another, communicating with one another while functioning somewhat interdependently. One simple way of defining differentiation is as an ability to be closely connected with just about anyone we choose and still be a self, still maintain a sense of one's own functional autonomy within the close relationship. It is the ability to be close to an emotionally important other while neither being dependent on gaining the other's acceptance and approval nor fearing the other's disapproval, rejection, or criticism of how we are. It is also being comfortable with the differences in the other person, particularly in times of higher anxiety, and not letting those differences cause emotional distance on our part. It means not needing to change the other to meet our expectations, or change ourselves to meet the other's, in order to be close.

Differentiation is a process that happens within a person as well as between people. Internally, it requires the ability to be aware of the difference between functioning on an emotional basis, where we are deeply connected to those in the emotional system around us, and functioning on an intellectual basis, where we are able to use our rationality to do our own more objective thinking. Most of us have this ability, to some extent, during times of lowered anxiety. The more we are able to do this in times of higher anxiety, the more likely it is that we have a higher level of differentiation.

Many of the stories about Jesus' encounters with the disciples, the crowds, and the Pharisees show us a man who did not let his emotionality take over and derail his ability to stay focused and to think clearly. The few times we see his anger, it is clearly a rational decision of his to show it. Surely, for example, he had gone by the Temple before and not made an issue of the commercial trade going on there. But at the time he chose to react, he engaged in a provocative and angry act that could only have been designed to elicit a strong reaction from the authorities. He knew what he was doing.

On the other hand, we see that Paul had to struggle more with his reactivity when he was under attack. Emissaries from the Jerusalem church and other factions came to the congregations he had started and preached a different gospel, questioning his leadership and authority. His energetic defensiveness was partly from a zeal for the gospel and partly a personal issue. His letters reveal a man who was attempting to keep a warm personal connection to those communities while also struggling with his anger with them.

Our subjective feeling-states at any given time, especially during times of higher anxiety, are not just about us; they mostly reveal our place and way of functioning in an emotional system. When we are controlled by our feelings, we operate from our perceptions of and experience in the emotional system. This includes what we think are the expectations of others within the system. We can comply with those expectations, rebel against them, fight and try to change them to fit our expectations, or simply try to distance from the system. Regardless of our response, however, our feelings are all about our relationship to the emotional systems to which we are connected.

As we grow up in our families, we develop some automatic reactions to the family system, and we take this reactivity into our adult life. These reactions will be the programmed emotional underlay to our functioning as pastors when the anxiety in the church system goes up. If we grew up in a better-differentiated family, we are more likely to have learned the skills of functioning at that level. If we grew up in a less well differentiated family, we will likely have more challenges to functioning competently in our adult life.

Being able to gain some emotional distance from these feelings and the associated reactivity means we are moving toward greater differentiation of self. We are separating a self out of the emotional conglomerate of the system. If, for example, we see someone or something as a threat to us in the system, rather than reacting automatically with the fight-or-flight response, we will be better able to evaluate whether a threat truly exists and, if so, to think about how best to respond for a positive outcome. People differ in their ability to do this. Those who do a better job of evaluating their responses tend to function more effectively as pastors and experience fewer difficulties in the long run, although they may occasionally initiate some short-term "difficulties" as a result of their differentiating moves.

The level of functional self is negotiable in emotional systems, meaning we can give or get self in relation to others. This is the outer aspect of differentiation. If, for example, we act as if others don't really measure up to us in their functioning, then we can bolster our sense of self with this belief. If others go along with this belief, then they give up self to us, and we function at a higher level than our basic self. This is our *functional level* of differentiation.

Many pastors and leaders gain self in this way. Their assigned role in the church as pastor gives it to them. People in the congregation defer to them, and they may appear to be more mature, confident, and stable than they really are. If people stop deferring, for whatever reason, the anxiety of these pastors will increase, and their underlying immaturity will begin to show. If they are charismatic and have a kind of mystique or aura around them, they can be seen as stronger leaders than they are. Or if they intimidate and frighten people, the same thing may happen.

The part of self that is negotiable within relationships is called *pseudo-self*. We can gain self by being a part of a social movement or cause, by being a part of some group that we or society hold in esteem, or by being in a hobby group, owning a particular car, eating at certain types of restaurants, cheering for a particular team (if they win, then "we are the greatest"; if they lose, "we are awful"), or doing any number of things that we think make us distinctive or important. All of us do this to some degree.

Marital partners are at the same basic level of differentiation. If they weren't, they probably wouldn't have gotten together or would not have stayed together for long. However, they may engage in so much over-functioning and underfunctioning negotiation of self over the years that one partner may look very competent and the other much less so. The more competent one has gained self from the other, who has given up self. If one partner dies, then the true level of self of the remaining partner will emerge. As pastors, we have often seen this happen with couples in our congregation.

Children normally have about the same level of differentiation as their parents, or, if they are the focus of the projection process, they will have a lower level, like my cousin Tom. These latter types of children will have more of their thinking, feeling, and behavior determined by the family relationship system. If they have been able to avoid at least some of this emotional focus while growing up and have been able to develop more on their own, they may have a bit higher level of differentiation than their parents. They will have more functional autonomy in relation to the emotional system, meaning that they can still stay connected but think, feel, and act more out of their own personal decisions about how to be. This often happens with the siblings of a child who was a focus of the projection process. The siblings are free to do better because the one focused on got so much anxious attention.

DEFINING A SELF

At the core of differentiation is the personal task of defining who we are within our emotional systems. The goal is to be a more solid self, which requires an ability to think more objectively for ourselves, to figure out what makes sense to us about who we are and what we want to do and be within the communities we belong to.

Defining a self means identifying the beliefs, values, commitments, and life principles on which we will base our life. These determine how we will or won't behave in every circumstance of life, and particularly within our closest relationships. To the extent that we do this, these core commitments become a part of our *solid self*, the part of self that we do not negotiate away in our relationships.

But when we compromise what we believe for the sake of "fitting in" or "going along" with the group or out of fear of losing a close relationship or simply out of a desire to reduce our level of anxiety and feel more secure and less threatened, then we are operating out of our pseudo-self. This is the part of us that is negotiable within emotional relationships. Peter's initial affirmations that Jesus is "the Christ" were clearly out of his pseudo-self. His affirmation of belief was not "rock solid." On the evening of Jesus' arrest, Peter denied even knowing him because he feared for his own life. If it is true that Peter died upside down on a cross in Rome because he would not renounce his faith, then he eventually made this faith a part of his more solid self. He eventually became more like the rock for which he was named.

Biblically, the part of us that I am calling "self" refers to our "heart." As we think in our hearts, so are we. The heart can be weak or strong, easily bent or rock solid. The heart is the center of volition in the person, and it can incline us to the things of life or to death. This is a central psychological image throughout the Bible. You will be amazed at how many references there are to the "heart" in your concordance. There are too many citations even to make a start here, but—for example—the Beatitudes are for the "pure in heart," and Paul tells us that obedience to God and faith are centered in the heart. The good news is about the receiving of a "new heart," which will allow us to be people of a solid and unshakeable faith and to act in ways that are consistent with God's love for the world.

Our hearts are shaped first of all in our families. We come by our strengths and our problems of the heart honestly. Our experience within that emotional system is where we first begin to create a sense of self and to determine how we will and won't behave. Being able to move beyond the reactivity and the negotiable aspects of self in that system, which is such a huge part of who we are, is a primary task of differentiation of self. Sometimes our family members have supported and promoted our differentiation of self through their own differentiation. This was symbolized for me when my mother gave me her apron strings when I turned twenty-one.

DIFFERENTIATION AND UNRESOLVED EMOTIONAL ATTACHMENT

We all come out of our families with some degree of unresolved emotional attachment, which affects our level of differentiation. We carry it with us wherever we go and whatever we do. The best hope for changing it is to go back to our family of origin, reconnect with members of that family, and work at defining ourselves better within the family. We can do the work in other arenas of life, but if we do it in our family of origin, we are going directly to the source of our issues.

A primary purpose of family of origin work is to better resolve this attachment. Some have never tried to do this. Their emotional existence, even as grown adults, remains tied up in their families. They have difficulty functioning independently of family and seem to have never left home. What the family thinks, feels, and wants is more important than having their own direction in life. For them, being a self seems wrong and "selfish." However, by compliantly giving up their own individuality, they are engaging in an underground kind of distancing from family. They are hiding their real selves. We know some people function this way in the church also.

More of us have tried to deal with family by some degree of emotional distancing or even cutoff when we left home. We thought, "Now I can be my own person." But it doesn't work that way. We become our own person by reconnecting with and working at being the self we avoided being while living with them. Most of us hesitate to do this. We fear getting trapped or swallowed up in that family system. The more resistant people are to doing family work, the more likely they are to be emotionally trapped in that system, even while keeping their distance. The fact is that we don't grow up and become mature by staying away from those people. We gain emotional separation and maturity by getting closer to them and working at being a self in their presence.

By gaining that kind of maturity, we can then think more clearly in the other powerful emotional systems we are a part of, such as the church. The more objectivity we can gain in a high-anxiety and intense emotional area like our families, the better we can function in these other systems. The work is about more than our families; it is about all of our lives and relationships. People who have worked at this in their families have reported that they did better at their jobs. Even people who were the heads of social or activity groups find they receive praise for the leadership they provide. One funny example is of a man who had done family of origin work and was told by members, "You are the best president of our handball association we have ever had."

On a larger social scale, for example, one of our responsibilities as Christians is to be good citizens. The better differentiated we are, the better citizens we can be. This is a difficult thing to do since getting accurate information through the media is not easy. We get handed a lot of groupthink based on the agendas of particular people and are told what we ought to think, feel, and do. Sometimes, our church community gets caught up in the groupthink. Greater differentiation will help us to assess more accurately what is truly a threat to us individually and as a society, and what we should do about the real threats we face. Much of the focus of our leaders and their use of the media is on things that are not truly a threat to us, but people allow their emotionality and anxieties to be stimulated and shaped by these distortions, and things that are really a threat are ignored until it is too late.

THREE THINGS THE WORK IS NOT ABOUT

1. Family of origin work is not about treating or changing our family.

Family of origin work is not about doing anything "to" our family. It is not a therapeutic technique for influencing or healing or enlightening families. Getting focused on trying to be a therapist to our families or to particular family members is one of the main reasons people fail at doing this work. This takes our focus off our own part in the family emotional system, and it continues the old reactive process that has gone on for as long as families have existed. Doing the work requires full respect for the individuality of all family members and the choices they have made. The work is not about confronting them or "getting all the feelings out," getting them to communicate better, being more supportive or closer and warmer, or getting them to "accept" us or "love" us or forgive us.

Differentiation means we can be a self without requiring other family members to be different in any way. If we see others as the source of our "unhappiness" or the means to achieving "happiness" if only they will be the way we want them to be, we are still caught up in the fusion of the emotional system. I once heard a well-known therapist in my town say over the radio, "The reason I have had two divorces is because I came from a dysfunctional family, and they messed me up." He saw them as the cause of his problems.

We want to take the focus off the problems of others, to stop diagnosing or labeling them, and to bring the focus back to our problems in relating. The effort is about defining a self within the emotional system, not defining others. This requires first understanding the normal functional processes of our family system, observing what part we play in the system, and then changing our part by better defining a self. The people in the system will each have their own reactions to that self-definition. They will most likely attempt to impede it and, if unsuccessful, then eventually will adjust to our new way of being in the system.

It is true that successfully improving our own level of functioning in the system will positively influence the system over time. Most people in the system will begin to do a bit better and be less problematic. Differentiation is a challenge to the level of functioning of others, and often they will pull up their own level in response. However, because the change is discomforting for them, others in the system will at first attempt to sabotage the self-definition and pull back the person's higher level of functioning. If the person doing the work can remain nonreactive and firm, then the others will adjust. The family cannot help benefiting from someone who is in close contact with them in times of higher anxiety and who is also less anxious and reactive, calmer, and clearer-thinking. Just by virtue of being in the presence of a stronger self, others are challenged to better define themselves.

However, we do not do this work in cooperation with others in the family or with their understanding and support. "We" do not differentiate; "I" do. So we keep our own counsel. We work alone. This may feel lonely for some, but that is the only way it can be done. If you find yourself taking others in the family into your confidence and trying to explain to them what you are up to, then you are still caught in the system. You are looking for their understanding, approval, and support. This inclination may come out of our anxiety around being different and making a change, but trying to get the cooperation of others misses the point. The only people who may know about your efforts in their entirety may be your coach or the group you have been working with.

A corollary to this is that family systems work is not about treating or changing our congregations. The biggest mistake I see people who begin to work with systems theory in their church make is that they see it as a tricky way to change a congregation. However, this work is about changing self while staying in relationship with others. How the others are going to be is up to them. It is not our job to make them different in any way. Any attempt to do so comes more out of our own fusion and unfinished business with our family.

2. Bowen theory is not antifeeling.

There are three types of subsystem functions within a person: the emotional system, the feeling system, and the intellectual system. Bowen's family of origin work is not antifeeling or anti-emotional or simply "intellectual." The words *feeling* and *emotion* mean different things in terms of the theory. Emotionality is the more all-encompassing word and refers to more than just our feelings. It includes our instincts and drives—for example, our autonomic functioning, most of which is beyond our awareness. Research has demonstrated how our blood pressure, skin temperature, and galvanic skin response go up and down during the seconds, minutes, and hours of our relationships with others, but we have no awareness of this. Our physical body is probably connected to our relationship system in ways we have not yet considered.

We share our emotional system with the rest of the animal creation. A great deal of similarity exists, in particular, between us and other mammals. In terms of our DNA, humans have nearly 99 percent of the same genes as chimpanzees. As Christians we are grown accustomed to focusing on how we differ from other animals, but we can learn much about ourselves by studying the animal world and what we have in common with it. The idea that we are wholly and completely separate from and unique compared to the animal world and the rest of creation is not very biblical. I think the creation stories emphasize how much we are a part of the rest of creation, and certainly our bodies, as they are created, share much in common with the animal world.

The feeling system is a combination of the emotional system and the intellectual system. It is that part of the emotional system that we more or less consciously experience and have labeled with different kinds of feeling words. The labeling comes from our intellectual system. Our feeling experience gets shaped and labeled most often within our families but also in other life experiences we have while growing up. People in a system can have different feelings when faced with similar challenges in their family or church. This makes the feelings subjective. They are more about us (as subject) than they are about the objective reality we face.

Besides being a minister and counselor, I am a ski instructor. If I were to take a group to the top of a tall mountain and have them point their skis over the edge of a cornice with a steep drop and then I were to say, "We are going down here," they would each experience an autonomic emotional event with very similar body chemistry, but the conscious feeling of each person would differ greatly. Some might have outright fear and freeze in place, saying, "I can't move." Some might compliantly say, "If you say so, boss," and then fall and tumble down the mountain and break something. Some might start feeling sad about missing their family when they die. Some might get angry with me for exposing them to this danger. Some might say, "Oh boy, let's get started!" We would all, some more than others, have extra adrenaline flowing in our system. We would just label that emotional experience differently depending on our personal and family history.

We humans appear to be unique in the animal world in our degree of being consciously aware of and labeling our feelings and even some of our emotionality. We can find some objectivity on our subjectivity. We can discover some of the processes that run us, even though more remains to be understood. That is the aim of Bowen theory.

But being able to label our feelings is minor compared to the challenge of understanding and gaining some control over our emotionality. It is our intellectual system that allows us even to attempt this act of labeling our experience. As far as we can tell, this uniquely human ability is truly extraordinary in comparison to the animal world. Some of the higher mammals—dolphins, whales, chimps, and apes—seem to be able, for example, to recognize themselves as themselves when they first encounter a mirror. They immediately begin to make faces as if they know they are doing it. But their ability to be objective does not appear to go too much further than this. Animals with less developed intellectual systems usually attack the image in the mirror as if it were an intruder. They cannot be "objective."

Our intellectual system is not entirely a free agent. The thinking part of our brain, the neocortex, is closely wired into the rest of the brain. Thus our rational thinking can be enlisted by our subjectivity so that we might never emerge from the purely emotional. Our thinking can be taken over by our irrational fears, feelings, and reactivity. This is part of the experience of fusion. It means we have a "fused" brain.

The close connection of the neocortex to the rest of the brain actually is a good thing. It is a survival mechanism that allows us to respond quickly in emergencies. The danger is that, in our emotional fusion, we can make situations into emergencies when they are not truly a threat. We must learn to recognize when we are doing this and be able to rise above it. We need to know that, on some occasions (for example, when facing an angry church member), what we feel or the beliefs we have chosen on the basis of our emotionality are not necessarily real. Growing up is a process of learning that, unlike the perception of children, our dreams are not real.

To the extent that our intellectual system is able to operate independently of our emotional system, we are better able to differentiate a self within that emotional system. The goal of this work is not to be less feeling or less emotional; rather, it is to be able to choose which system we will operate out of at any one time. It is to be able to step outside of the emotional system, look at self in context and, like the chimps with a mirror, decide how we will move our face and, more important, our lives. In being able to move toward greater objectivity, we can learn to describe the world and our relationships more as they are, rather than as we "feel" them to be.

So family systems theory is also about our emotionality, an emotionality that we will never be rid of—and don't want to be rid of. It is what connects us to one another, allowing us to be sensitive and compassionate and caring when we choose to be. Michael Kerr tells a story about Bowen and himself that illustrates the importance of connection for Bowen. Kerr had finished his psychiatric residency with Bowen and went off to work in another town. When he was leaving Georgetown, he told Bowen, "I'll be in touch." Months went by, and Bowen heard nothing from him. Finally, Bowen wrote to him and simply said, "If this is how you 'stay in touch' then no wonder you are having trouble with your family."

It is good to be aware of our feelings, and even to be able to express them when need be, and not to repress them. But it is not useful to let them run us and to feel compelled to express them whenever the urge hits us (such as when facing that angry church member). Contrary to some psychological theories, such actions are not healthy. Behind our negative feelings in our relationships is anxiety, the issue we need to focus on and develop an ability to manage. That is a part of what differentiation is about. As we change our way of functioning in the system, our feelings will change. That is guaranteed.

3. Bowen theory is not antitogetherness.

The idea that Bowen theory is antitogetherness comes out of the juxta-position of individuality and togetherness in the theory. But together-ness, like emotionality, goes with the territory of being human. It is not something about which we have any choice. We are highly social ani-mals; even hermits are caught up in togetherness issues just by virtue of vehemently rejecting and rebelling against society.

Individuality involves our ability to exercise emotional autonomy within an emotional system. It is not about cutting off from that system or not needing it. To say, "I don't need other people," is a pseudo-independent stance, and we are fooling only ourselves. In fact, the more individuality or emotional autonomy we have, the more capable we are of getting close to and connecting with others. It is just that our thinking, feeling, and behav-ior will be less determined by what others expect and more by what makes sense to us, based on our beliefs and values. When we are more confident about our individuality, we are less threatened by others and more com-fortable with getting close, even with that angry church member. Getting close doesn't mean somebody has to give up self.

Differentiation of self is a process that allows us to better manage the togetherness force that is a part of all of life. From my perspective, God is about both togetherness and individuality. God is both well con-nected to creation and highly individual in relation to it. We would not have community without togetherness, and the healthiest communities have more individuality. Emotionally separate and autonomous people make for better, healthier togetherness in community.

A THEOLOGICAL NOTE

No one has succeeded in fully differentiating a self. Perhaps Jesus comes the closest to it. To engage in anthropomorphism a bit, I suppose that God is the ultimate in terms of differentiation—and perhaps even God had to develop these skills in relation to creation. One could read the Bible that way when it speaks of God "repenting of his" reactivity to human corruption.

But the scale of differentiation and fusion is not about the doctrine of salvation. Differentiation is not the way to salvation as in a kind of works righteousness. We can all be saved no matter what our level of dif-ferentiation is. We can all receive God's grace no matter how fused and problematic we are. This goes for the members of our family as well. That is the good news of the gospel.

I place the kind of growth that comes with differentiation of self within the doctrine of sanctification rather than the doctrine of justification. It is about us cooperating with the Holy Spirit to become healthier (which for me also means "better") people. Differentiation allows us to move toward becoming the kind of human beings God created us to be.

The theory offers us a concrete way of becoming the kind of Christians we are exhorted to become in the Bible. I see the Bible as holding up the values and ethical principles that require the emotional maturity of differentiation of self to achieve. These are not achievable without that emotional maturity. Through faith, prayer, and the guidance of the Holy Spirit, the theory gives us the means to grow. Thus the theory has become part of my ethical thinking, even though Bowen probably did not intend this. But in so doing, as with any other approach to health, I—and we—have to avoid making it into a moralistic program that people must subscribe to. This would entirely miss the point.

Paul spoke of being in the world but not of it. This could be a way of speaking about differentiation in the emotional system of our families. How do we remain in good emotional contact with our family and remain outside of it, so that we are not run by it and, without reflection, take on its values and beliefs or simply react to the people in it? In my thinking, Paul and Bowen were on the same wavelength here.

As Christians we recognize that we are a people of history. God encounters us in the reality of history. Part of our own personal history is in our family of origin, and we need to honor what God has given us in this part of our history. To be able to embrace our family without needing to make them different, or react to them, or cut off from them, whatever their level of functioning may be, is a part of how we honor God. I believe that we need to know and be able to tell our family story as a part of building up the community of God. We will be healthier pastors and a healthier church for it.

6

READINESS TO DO THE WORK

Learning the concepts of family systems theory is usually the first step in doing family of origin work. The titles listed in the bibliography provide a good start. However, the crucial step of learning to "think systems" will not really come from that reading or even from hearing the concepts discussed. That ability will come slowly, as we are in the midst of our family system and see the concepts at work there. Once we begin to see and think of our family as a reciprocal, interactive emotional system, our understanding of family functioning will change. We will see our family and our participation in it in a new way. We need patience and time. Everyone "gets it" in different ways, but it is noticeable when it happens. It is definitely an "Aha, so that's how it works" moment.

In addition, we need to work on certain early steps as a part of our beginning work in family. Early visits to family can just be about working on these steps, and nothing more. They will be change enough. How we go about accomplishing these steps, or at least getting started on them, is up to us. We might want to have a coach or a family of origin group who understands what is needed and can mentor us along the way. They will help us to achieve greater objectivity about our family.

1. LETTING GO OF EXPECTATIONS OF FAMILY MEMBERS

Normally, we are very aware of and sensitive to what family members expects of us. We tend to be less aware of what we expect of them—for example, "They shouldn't have any expectations of me." With this mindset, when going home and encountering one of their expectations, we react because we think, "They shouldn't do that." An implicit thought of ours that they "shouldn't say those things or be that way" sets us up for reactivity to them.

We can count on the fact that our family members are going to behave as they always have. We don't go back to family with the idea that they should have changed by now. In fact, for us to be able to do our work, they need to be the same. If they are on eggshells and cautious with us, it will slow us down. We will all just be "nice" with one another.

We can be as unrealistic in our expectations of family members as they can be of us. Instead of focusing on their part, we need to focus on letting go of our expectations of them. The work is not about changing them; rather, it is about changing us with them. One goal of the work is to better understand their expectations and to see the context for them more clearly. This usually involves our parents' own family of origin experience. When they express an expectation, we can learn something about them. If we are busy reacting to the expectation, however, we won't learn anything new.

Another goal is to focus on our part in how the emotional system of the family functions. We are not simply passive recipients of what our parents expect. We are also actors and reactors. It is not just a one-way street, a case of what the parents have done to the children. Everyone influences everyone else. How this works is not always obvious, but it will become so as we learn to be observers in the system. Having expectations also keeps us in an other-focused stance, characterized by our looking at them rather than at our own functioning. Our internal insistence that "they should be different" will keep us from being able to observe more objectively and research how our family emotional system functions.

I had no idea that my involvement as an inner-city pastor would have kept me from getting the story of my uncle Wallace's depression and death. That involvement became an expectation for my mother and aunt about how they should be around me, and they didn't want to address the topic. We need to understand that our family members can feel defensive with us and be reactive to what they think we expect, whether they are accurate or not. Parents can be quite sensitive to the accusations of their children. If you are a parent, you know this. Remember it is also true of our parents. It is difficult for any parent not to feel defensive when their grown child points out their mistakes.

If we are hung up on how critical our mother is of us, for example, and we can focus only on trying to get her to stop doing this, the work won't go anywhere. I ask people who feel this way, "What would it take for you to not hear your mother as being critical?" Then after the normal response of "What?" and repeating the question, we work at ways, first, to be less sensitive to the criticism and, then, to stop hearing it as criticism. Again, each person does it differently.

One adult woman couldn't stop hearing her father criticize and then reacting, no matter what she did. She knew he was speaking more out of his own vulnerability and fears when he focused his negativity on her, but this didn't help. Finally, she discovered, on her own, that a slightly hostile image helped her. Whenever he was "criticizing" her, she imagined a raw egg breaking over his head. She found the image so humorous that it helped to interrupt the reactivity. Eventually, she didn't need the image.

One younger, unmarried woman complained of her mother's criticisms, some of which focused around her not yet being married. She worked at a way that she could hear the comments as her mom's expression of concern for her, coming out of her own anxieties. With each criticism she learned to thank her mom for her concern and then asked about how her mom became aware of the issue for herself. "Who told her about the concern?" "When did she first realize it and do something about it in her own life?" "Was it difficult for her?" "How did she get to be so good at it?" "How had her mother been with her on this issue?" "Did she ever 'lose it' with her mother?" "Or did she ever fail at managing the concern?"

This woman did a good job with these questions in response to her mother's criticisms, and it changed the nature of the interaction between the mother and daughter. Her mother became a lot more open with her. She learned a lot about her mother, and her mother began to back off of the criticisms. The question of "How did she get to be so good at (the issue) herself?" really slowed her mother down. She didn't think she was good at it, and she wanted her daughter to be better than she was. This opened up a lot of territory for discussion about the mother's life.

The daughter turned the criticisms into a research opportunity for getting to know her mom better. The atmosphere between them improved considerably, but then she almost lost it once at the airport. Shortly before she was to board her plane (beware the airport "good-bye" scenes), her mother said to her, "You know dear, men like fuller figured women, and your breasts are rather small. You might consider doing something about them." She was feeling so good and slightly smug about the visit, thinking that this was now a dead issue, that she was caught off guard. But she recovered enough to move toward her mom and put her arm around her and say, "Thank you, mom, for your concern. I know you would like for me to get married some day. But I happen to like my little breasts, and, actually, so do the men I have dated. Good-bye. I love you." As she got on the plane, she felt as if she had just barely escaped.

In my own case I was so busy being resentful that my mother was not asking questions and being interested in me that I rarely volunteered anything to her about my life. Reactively, I just stayed focused on what she wasn't doing, and feeling quietly angry. In fact, it turned out she was interested but wanted me to volunteer information since she didn't want to pry or be intrusive like her own stepmother. I was saying to myself, "She isn't being a mother to me," rather than thinking, "I am not treating her like a mother."

Lowering expectations of others is what makes closeness and connection possible. Raising your expectations of others will create defensiveness and distancing. To better connect with family members, we have to let go of our expectations of them and be interested in their expectations. Saying this, I know that a certain percentage of readers are going to focus on their family members and say, "See, that is why I stay so distant from them and don't tell them who I am. Their expectations are so high." They will use these thoughts to justify themselves and blame their family. It is difficult not to slip into an other-focus. Do your best to apply these thoughts to yourself rather than to them. If you are reactive to them, you also have expectations of them. That is where your work needs to focus.

If we want to get people to distance from us, we need only to raise our expectations of them. Ninety percent of the time, when parents refuse to answer their children's questions, this is the issue. The parents fear the judgment and criticism of their adult children. Most people are not aware of how much influence they have on their parents.

Having expectations of others is part of how we make things safe for ourselves. We can look at their "inadequacies" and react to those rather than just be with our own vulnerabilities. By their continuing to act as they always have, we can say, "They will never change. They are just the way I remember them. What is the point of doing this?" This will automatically lead to failure in our family work. How can we listen to and interact with our family without needing them to be different from how they are? That is our challenge.

Church leaders who hold on to expectations of their parents are more likely to collude with factions in their church and repeat the patterns there. Their expectations of others will create distance and separatism and help keep the church stuck. Of course, the people we collude with think of us as empathetic and supportive, or even as a powerful and bold leader, but such a triangle does not help the church.

I see clergy getting themselves into trouble when they develop firm expectations for their church or for particular members or committees or functions. One area where this can be played out is around budgets. If the clergy think the church budget is "theirs" and ought to reflect their own priorities and goals, this often sets them up for a head-on clash with someone whose "turf" they are invading. In modern society, money is an extension of the old territoriality instinct. If we make plans for "their" money, we are infringing on their territory and are likely to get an angry reaction. This can lead to fights and possibly the clergy person getting fired.

This phenomenon is not restricted to the clergy. One committee can infringe on the traditional territory of another, and a fight may ensue. Territoriality goes deep into our biological and emotional systems. We can all be reactive to intrusions from others. We can preach being "a good Christian" in these circumstances, but we are up against some very powerful, long-established emotional system forces.

Enlarging or shrinking or otherwise changing the boundaries of the territory is always slow and difficult work, unless you want to have all-out war or attempt to pull off a coup. The fallout from such activity can be a heavy price and often not worth it. Working on modifying or reducing your expectations and how you will function around these emotional realities is the best route to take in most cases.

2. LOWERING REACTIVITY

Reactivity takes so many different forms that it would be impossible to list them all here. Nearly every sort of problematic behavior is most likely a form of reactivity to family. Besides the four basic patterns I listed in chapter 2, we can be cold and indifferent or emotionally insensitive to others. We can be hostile and provocative. We can go out of control and become violent or aggressive, or act out sexually, or develop addictions. We can be abusive or manipulative or simply intrusive and disrespectful. Some forms of caring, rescuing, and overfunctioning can also be reactive patterns. Always giving help and never asking for it or just giving support and advice can also be reactivity. Nearly all of these reactions help to create reactivity in others.

Having our own expectations of family members, or focusing just on their expectations, leads us to react to family. That is what we learned to do growing up, and doing so as adults will continue the circular pattern of interaction that goes nowhere. We cannot do family of origin work while we are still highly reactive to our family. All reactivity involves some form of distancing from others when feeling unsafe. The issue is how to move closer to others.

We have to find a way to manage our anxiety and sense of threat. A good start is to begin to discover the areas in which our anxiety emerges and we get reactive. We can then develop a plan for how to keep our level of anxiety down. What are our best methods for keeping our cool and not slipping into reactivity? This is a good practice to work at perfecting. One way is to see how we could make ourselves be more reactive; how could we accentuate the patterns rather than subdue them? If we really wanted to go over the top, what would we have to do?

Too many therapists and pastors who counsel tend to side with their clients' reactivity to their parents. They collude with the distancing and cutoff, probably because they have done the same thing with their families. Conversely, some take the parents' side and try to get the client to "understand" the parents, maybe to be forgiving of them and whatever wrongs that happened. This also will not lead to change.

A colleague of mine describes one of his students saying he was "ready to go home and differentiate" himself in his family. He always got a kick when someone would say something like this to him. People were showing their lack of understanding of the concept and how much work it took. When the student got back from his trip home, my friend asked how it went. The student said, "Terrible." He was a smoker, and as soon as he could after getting off the plane, he lit up. His parents had met him at the airport, and when he took out his cigarettes, his mother said, "I see you are still a smoker." He instantly said, "I'm a grown man. I can do what I want." He didn't recover from his adolescent, rebellious reaction for the rest of the visit. He couldn't get out of the old circular perception of seeing them trying to control him and showing them they couldn't.

A man I worked with had a history of being rebellious with his parents. He came to see me because he was getting in trouble in his workplace over similar kinds of issues with his superiors. When it began to be obvious to him, without my telling him, that family was where he could best deal with this issue, he took it on. His family visits often ended early in some kind of blowup, with their criticizing him and demanding that he change and his then yelling at them and storming out of the house. While his reactions were not quite as extreme in his workplace, he saw the relevance of his family emotional system patterns to interactions at work.

We carefully worked at how he could avoid this pattern and experiment with being different in his family. He did well with it and had several visits that did not end in a blowup or a shouting match. He was also able to begin to learn some things about his parents. However, he sensed that they were somehow uncomfortable with this new experience.

On another visit, one morning after not having slept well, he got up early, before his parents. He was standing looking out the window, drinking his coffee. Then his parents came in and gave one of their cheery "Good mornings." He swore something back at them about it being a "lousy morning" and told them to "back off" with their cheery good mornings. Then he thought he had blown it. But his parents, in a kind of delighted way, both exclaimed, "There's the son we have always known and loved."

Then he got it. His rebellion had played a role for them. He gave them something to focus on other than themselves and their relationship, which was uncomfortable for them. They could diagnose and treat him rather than deal with their own lives. He began to think that over the years of growing up he had sacrificed getting on with his own life and development by drawing attention to his screwups and immaturity so that they, at some level, could feel safer and less anxious about their own lives. Then he was less anxious. It didn't matter to him that he was often "in trouble" as a result.

Now he was beginning to "think systems." Then he noticed something else. Within a year of his moving out of the house, his parents had invited his aunt, his mom's younger, several-times-divorced sister, to move in with them. He had always thought this strange because they didn't really seem to like her. She had not done well in her life, and, for a portion of his visits, they would complain to him about her smoking and drinking and the men she dated and how she wasn't doing anything useful with her life. He saw that his aunt had stepped right into his old position in the household.

Seeing all of this helped him establish a more proactive focus in his own life. He got less caught up in the expectations of others and became less reactive. His relationships at work improved, as did his relationship with the woman he was dating. But these were not things I could have told him. He had to think them through for himself in response to my verbal musings and wonderings. It really was no big deal to me if he changed and did family work or not. He didn't have to rebel against me. I was just impressed with his sacrifice of his own life by focusing on the expectations of others.

Doing this work, and being different with our family, can create a certain amount of tension for everyone for a while. If we stop doing our reactive patterns, people will notice. There will be efforts to draw us back in. In the case of this young man, the effort was not intense because they had his aunt on which to focus. However, they could have upped the pressure on him by criticizing him more heavily.

In some cases the changes we make will lead family members to wonder if something is wrong with us. If we are no longer compliant and "obedient," they may say we don't love or care for them anymore or that we are not as nice as we used to be. Siblings may say that we are upsetting our parents and tell us to "stop doing it." Dad might say we are going to give Mom a heart attack if we keep on being so "obstinate and uncaring."

Being less reactive is an important step in the differentiating process. The feelings that people experience around this reflect the emotional process of the family. We have to go counter to the feelings we experience at these points. It may be something like "this doesn't feel right" or "normal." It's true; it is not "normal." But this is part of letting go of the old automatic patterns of the past. Our trained responsiveness to one another took a long time to develop, and we are trying to create something new for ourselves.

The reactions of others to our lowered reactivity can throw us off course. As they up the ante and try to evoke our old reactions, thus keeping the system stabilized and themselves less anxious, we will be tempted back into our old patterns. We will have to think ahead about how we will stay on course when they react to our changes. We have thought through about how to be less reactive in the old way, but then we may "expect" that they understand and appreciate our changes. Can't they see the good thing we are trying to do for the family? We might even feel tempted to explain it to them. Don't. It won't do the job. We are not looking for their cooperation and acceptance or praise. Coming to terms with us is their job. We just stay focused on our direction.

Reactivity to the expectations of church members is another way that clergy get themselves in trouble. Whatever headway we can make on being less reactive in family will give us a solid boost to achieving the same thing in the church.

3. DEVELOPING GREATER OBJECTIVITY

If we are able to make progress on the first two steps of lowered expectations and lowered reactivity, then we are likely developing greater objectivity about our family and about our place and functioning in it. As we develop this emotional objectivity, we will become more curious. Curiosity about family processes is our best clue that this objectivity is taking hold.

Differentiation requires greater awareness of the dual emotional processes at work both in our family emotional system and within us. In gaining the kind of emotional detachment that comes with learning to manage our reactivity, and in developing greater objectivity, we will be less determined by those family emotional processes. But we will also make better emotional contact with people because of our greater awareness. In developing objectivity we will be deprogramming ourselves from the emotional system. We will be more aware of "how" we are in it and how we think about how we want to be in it, but less determined by its processes. This is not the same as emotional distancing. Distancing means we are still being run by the emotional system.

We can all be most objective about our family functioning when we are not "in" it. After our visit home is over, often we can see how we got caught and did the same old reactive thing. The point is how to bring the clarity we develop in hindsight into our present sight, during the visit, to see it when it is happening and to function accordingly. We want to defuzz our thinking while we are "in" the system, so that we can be less "of" the system.

Once we get to know the family patterns and our own reactions, it will help to have a plan for how we will do our part differently when the pattern kicks in. It is not just an issue of "what won't we do"; it is also an issue of "what will we do?" If we don't achieve our goal the first few times, we have to think about what we are missing. It takes time, patience, and repeated efforts. We are attempting to lay down new pathways in our brain that will interrupt the automatic reactivity of the old patterns. This is not easy work, but it can be done.

Another way to picture objectivity is as going up to the very top row of the football stadium and looking down on the playing field from up there. It is much easier to see the whole field and each team member's movement around a play. This is a lot different from being down on the field, in the midst of the action, and having so many people block your line of sight. We have to be able to do both. We have to be able to be down on the field in the action, in the game, and also have a sense of what it looks like from up high, seeing the whole thing.

What vantage point gives you this view of your church system? How far away do you have to get before you can see the whole thing and how each part, or each key player, moves? How do you manage to lose touch with this vision as you reenter the church doors? What can you do to keep that image fresh in your head as you are there, interacting with the players, being aware of everyone on the field, including yourself?

Having expectations for how the members of the congregation "ought" to be sets us up for being reactive rather than more objective. If we can keep our sense of how the larger system functions (not how we want it to function) and then have expectations only for how we will move during the action, our level of reactivity will automatically decrease. If we find ourselves fuming over a church meeting or an encounter with a church member, then we aren't there yet. Our family work can be a resource for learning how to change our part in the congregational emotional system.

4. SELF-FOCUS

Self-focus is what we have to keep coming back to. Self-focus means being able to stop watching what others are doing, to see if they are changing yet, and pay more attention to what we are doing in reaction to them. Doing this, we can begin to claim more responsibility for our part in the process; with that comes self-control.

People who feel deprived in their families, who think that their parents have not loved or cared for or listened enough to them, seem to have the biggest difficulties with self-focus. They have tried and tried to get these attentive behaviors from their parents, but the more they try to get it or accuse their parents of failing to give it, the more distant or defensive the parents become and the more deprived the people feel. It is an unending cycle. In my case, I never told my mother that she should ask me questions and show some interest; instead, I would wait and see and then feel distant and hold a grudge if she didn't. It took me a while to see my part in this and what I wasn't doing.

I repeat this because it is so common. Many people decide not to do family work because they think it is about changing their family members. They say, "What's the point? They will never change." We don't make family visits to see if they have changed yet. The idea of changing self within the family is a difficult thing to grasp. It often seems like a concession to "them." People ask, "Why should I be the one who has to change? They are the ones with the problems. The way things are is their fault, not mine."

A certain number of pastors have done the same thing in the church. They have taken a few of the family systems concepts and applied them to church members rather than to themselves. They attempt to use the concepts to "treat" the church and its members. Again, this work is not about changing others. It is about changing self. If any change happens in others, it will happen as a result of changing self, but we just have to forget that part of the statement and not focus on it or keep looking over our shoulder to see if it has happened yet.

Taking responsibility for our own part in the emotional process of the family is the way to emotional maturity. Denying responsibility for ourselves gives the system power over us. As long as we keep seeing "them" as responsible for our difficulties or unhappiness in life, we will stay stuck. If we think that we can't change until they change, then we are hopeless. If, instead, we can keep thinking, "Am I being the person I want to be in this situation, according to my best beliefs, values, and intentions?" we will be on the road of growth. It gets us out of the reactive position to the more proactive one of defining self rather than being defined by the system.

7

SIX PRINCIPLES
FOR REENTERING OUR FAMILY

There are no set, hard-and-fast strategies or rules for doing family of origin work. There are no specific techniques that guarantee success. Having a sound grasp of the theory is the best technique. With the theory in mind, each person reenters the family with a new understanding and awareness of what the family is about. The steps outlined in this chapter develop differently for each person.

What I offer here are some general directions for the work. What order they happen in or whether they all happen at once will vary. Unexpected experiences will occur, and at times it may seem as if there is just one obstacle after another. Things don't always happen the way we plan, and, after all, adaptability and flexibility are part of what we are trying to learn. In better-differentiated families the overall process will generally go more smoothly, but this is a rarity for most of us.

1. MAINTAINING ACTIVE, INTENTIONAL, REGULAR CONTACT

It seems paradoxical to some people that the way to greater freedom from family is to maintain regular contact with family. By now we should have discovered that emotional distancing doesn't do it. This work is much more than just visiting relatives and talking about the history of their family relationships. That is only one means for getting to the important issues of defining a self, but it is a very important means that has value in itself.

If time, distance, and money allow, frequent shorter visits every few months are better than longer, less frequent visits. Once I got started in the work, I found that I didn't mind the extra cost and time. In my case, two to three days was a good length for a visit. Some people say that twenty-four hours is their limit. A few people may be able to go longer. It works best if we go on our own rather than taking our partner and children with us. When they come along, then too many agendas are involved, and it is harder to develop the objectivity we need if, for example, our partner is there saying, "I thought you said you weren't going to do that anymore." I don't mean that we should never take our partner and children, but we should be sure to have some visits on our own.

It helps to have some personal plan for what we want to accomplish in a visit. Our intentional plan can include what relationship we would like to work at, information we would like to get, or how we would like to be in response to particular kinds of behaviors from others. The more we have done this, the better prepared we will be for the unexpected things for which we cannot plan. As we accomplish more successful visits, in terms of our personal goals for self, the whole system will adjust and often like what is happening. People will often look forward to our visits, and they may have been thinking about our questions and coming up with more information. They may begin to see us as a resource in their own lives.

However, we need to keep our plans to ourselves. Even if someone in the family has a sense of what he or she thinks we are doing and is very sympathetic, don't develop a coalition with that person. This is our unique individual work, not anyone else's. We all have our own work to do.

A general goal of this work is to be more a part of our family. As Murray Bowen said, it is "to be present and accounted for" in our family. Ideally, we can begin this work during periods of lower anxiety in the family. That makes for the easiest reentry. Learning to be present and accounted for is like money in the bank on which we can draw during times of higher anxiety. Those higher anxiety times are when we particularly want to be present. It sends a powerful message to family when we are willing to be there during the harder times. This is when some of the best family work is done, especially if we have caused the tension because of our attempts at differentiation.

Our differentiating moves will generally raise anxiety in the family, and particular members may be very reactive. They may tell us we are wrong, to go back to how we used to be, or they may lay out negative consequences if we don't change back. This is normal, since differentiating moves upset the emotional balance of the system. If we have some practice being in the family during times of higher anxiety, when the focus is not on us, this will help to desensitize us to the reactions when they are focused on us.

2. GETTING TO KNOW THEM BETTER

We want to be able to get a more objective sense of family functioning during times of higher anxiety and how we function within the family during these times. If we can be less reactive, avoid distancing, and stay connected with everyone, then we can begin to think about the family emotional process more clearly. Reactivity is our anxious response to a perceived threat. If we can lower our level of anxiety and feel less threatened when with family, then we can be more objective about the emotional process.

What is it that we feel we need to do to feel safer during the higher anxiety times? We may become angry and blame, or feel hopeless and fall apart, or get stubborn and resentful, or any number of things. Reactivity tends to stem from our sense of vulnerability and hurt, or a sense of potential loss. If we can be sensitive to these issues lying behind others' reactivity, then we won't have to react to them. When we have learned how to stay and be less anxious and more attentive to what is happening, then we have made a fundamental shift in the work.

I had begun my family work a couple of years before my mother had a brief separation from her fourth husband, Mike. He was in treatment for his alcoholism, and she called to let me know she was moving out. The reason did not have to do with his drinking. I said I was going to come right down to Los Angeles from Vancouver to help her with the move. That was a really important experience for her to know that I would be there in the tougher times. I learned some more about her as well, as we talked about the times she had done this before, leaving other men. I was also able to keep contact with Mike during an upsetting time for him. There was a time when previously I would have gone underground and been hard to reach during events like this.

During our visits home we have to spend individual time alone with each family member. In some families, trying to split up our parents for time alone with each one can be a real challenge. They say, "Well, why do you want to do that? We can talk with you just as well together. We don't have any secrets from one another, do we, dear?" If we haven't spent time alone with each of them before, we may have some difficulty getting this to happen. We may think they are the resistant ones, but it could be us.

I find a straightforward explanation of wanting to get to know each one alone is best. They could say, "What's to know? I am just the same as I always was. You've known me all these years. What are you up to?" You could say something like "I have always known you as Mom and Dad, like you were one unit joined at the hip. I'd like to get to know you a little better individually. Would you help me with this?" Asking for their "help" with this project often gets their cooperation, even though they may grumble about it.

Letter writing is a good way to prepare for visits. Try writing to just one parent rather than "Dear Mom and Dad." My mother knew something was up when I started writing letters on a more regular basis after spending most of my life being out of contact. I used the letters to help set the direction for what I wanted to do in a visit. I would raise things I wanted to talk about. My aunt didn't like to write letters, so I sent her questions in a letter along with a blank cassette tape for her to record her answers. She thought that was fine. This gave her a chance to think about my questions as well.

Once when Mom was coming up to visit me, I wrote a letter asking her if she would be willing to be recorded on videotape with me asking her questions. I told her the tape was something I would probably want to use in my training program with students. I gave her a list of some questions I would like to talk with her about, some of which were pretty tough. When I began the tape, I asked her, having seen the questions I wanted to ask, what did she think of them? She said, "They sound pretty nosey." I asked if that was OK, and she said, "I guess so." Remember her history of being asked questions by her mother. She then moved right into the experience and seemed to enjoy it.

Who are the most important family members for us to get to know better first? Relationships with parents are the normal starting point for most people, unless they involve a very difficult history that requires working at this more slowly. After the parents come relationships with siblings, grandparents, aunts and uncles, and cousins. Any progress you make in any relationship will be a plus for you, and the more relationships you work at, the better.

3. DEVELOPING A MULTIGENERATIONAL FAMILY DIAGRAM

When I began my work, I drew up a family diagram covering as much as I knew about the various generations of my family. It went back to my great-grandparents on my mother's side, but there were lots of blanks, missing dates, and people I didn't know anything about. I put in any of the dates of birth, death, marriage, and divorce that I had.

Then I sent off copies of this diagram to various family members and asked them for any information that was missing about people, relationships, dates, and so forth. I included a letter explaining that I had "become interested in learning more about my family and who we are" and "would you help me?" I briefly explained how the diagram works, including the meaning of the circles and squares and the various dates, and told them they could mark up the diagram or do whatever they wanted to do to correct it and give me more information.

In some cases I got more than I asked for, with somewhat confusing family trees going a long way back but no one knowing anything about the people on it. In other cases I received what is called "free information,"

FAMILY DIAGRAM SYMBOLS

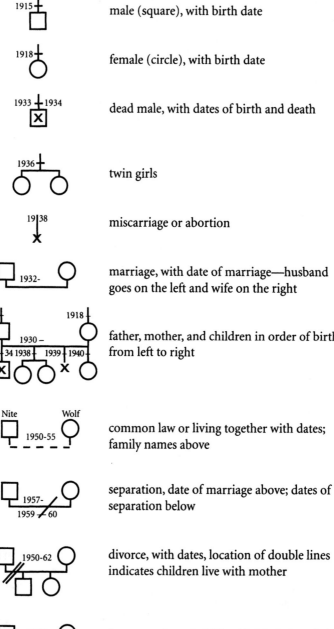

1915 — □   male (square), with birth date

1918 — ○   female (circle), with birth date

1933 — ⊠ — 1934   dead male, with dates of birth and death

1936 ○ ○   twin girls

19|38 ✗   miscarriage or abortion

□ 1932- ○   marriage, with date of marriage—husband goes on the left and wife on the right

1915 □   1930 –   1918 ○   father, mother, and children in order of birth from left to right
1930—34 1938 1939—1940
⊠ ○ ○ ✗ ○

Nite □ 1950-55 Wolf ○   common law or living together with dates; family names above

□ 1957- 1959—60 ○   separation, date of marriage above; dates of separation below

□ 1950-62 ○   divorce, with dates, location of double lines indicates children live with mother
□ ○

□ 1963 ○   foster or adopted child, with birth dates below and date of entering family above
1957

a volunteered comment about particular people. This information can lead directly into further inquiry through a visit or a telephone call.

I developed an enlarged family diagram as a result of this process. I took special note of where vagueness or incomplete information about particular people or relationships or dates still existed. For instance, I never was able to track down the story of one grand-uncle's move from Missouri to Oregon, where he had little contact with his family. He was the oldest of four boys in his family, and his seemed a strange and intriguing story. I have one picture of him with a dead deer wrapped around his shoulders and a rifle in one hand. I was able to eventually find and get in touch with his sixty-five-year-old son in Oregon, but he knew little about his father's family of origin or the reason he moved from Missouri. He was the only person in the family to move away from Missouri before my mother did. This cutoff has remained unsolved and unaddressed except for my contact with the son.

A multigenerational study of the family going back many generations can be helpful, but I would not suggest it as part of the early work. This would make it seem to people that we are just doing genealogy or family-tree work. However, over time it can be useful to see how various branches of the family have managed their own family emotional process. It can help us think about what generational lines of the family appear to have done better and what parts have not done as well. This will help clarify the origins of the strengths and liabilities in our own nuclear family.

4. HONORING THE FAMILY

People liked it when I could bring any information about distant relatives back to the more immediate family, and this further stimulated their own interest. Some people may not want to give particular information, such as with my uncle Wallace. People will remember the questions even when they don't answer them. The questions may burn away within them, and a pressure may build. When they feel safe with us and how we are using the information we gather, they may eventually offer a response.

In gathering this information we must be sure to demonstrate to people that we are interested in honoring family. We are not out "to get the dirt." We want to know everything about them, not just the "bad stuff." It will become clear to our family members that we are interested not in distinguishing the saints and sinners, but in understanding the real people of the family. This includes everyone's personal triumphs as well as difficulties. Both my mother and my aunt had lots of positive memories of their brother Wallace. We talked about these, and I shared the positive stories I could remember about him. I should have known that their vagueness around his depression was a sign of anxiety and a clue to go slow. I think my respect for him and my willingness to drop the topic helped them become comfortable with eventually telling me.

Another way of honoring the people we talk with is by listening respectfully when they tell us stories about themselves or others that don't fit with what we think we know. We don't challenge these stories or argue about them, even if we have heard contradictory stories from someone else or we "know for a fact" what happened because we were there. These stories are about *their* experience of their relationships with the people involved and what they may have had to do to manage themselves in those relationships. They may have to change the facts in order to feel more comfortable. Or maybe we have changed the facts in our own memory. When members of the family have quite different stories to tell about others, themselves, or a relationship, let that be a clue about the family emotional process.

People are often amazed at how differently their own siblings see the family and how different their memories are. They will say, "Are we talking about the same family here?" Well, in a sense, they aren't. Each sibling is born into a different family. The family constellation is different with each new birth. And as time passes, the family itself evolves. It becomes a different kind of organism. Thus it is inevitable that each child's memories of events will be different, so take that as a gift for getting another perspective on the family system.

My latest version of the family diagram would go with me on all my visits, and I would bring it out at the first chance of spending some time alone with people. We would look at it together, and I would ask questions and listen to their stories. Their stories would lead to more questions on my part, and we would get further into the history of relationships and how they managed them. This was a good way to get a relationship going with each individual member of the family and to talk with them about their experience of family. Some hesitated initially, but that was soon overcome when they saw that I respected their information; after that, they would look forward to my visits. The connections developed in this process proved invaluable for the critical events to come.

In the visits I would ask if they knew anything about the circumstances of each birth. In my mother's case, in particular, this was crucial, with her own mother's death occurring so closely after her birth. We were able to confirm that my mom's mother had not been doing well physically for a couple of years before Mom's birth, and this helped Mom feel less guilty about her death. So it is useful to get information about deaths (what people died of, the history of the illness, who seemed most affected by the death, what changed in the family after the death, how were these changes managed by different members of the family, and so forth), marriages, divorces, and the history of their work life, their hopes and dreams and accomplishments and failures. If people had gone to university or gotten a higher education, I would ask about that. In each case, what we are looking for is not just the basic information and dates but also how the emotional process of the family developed from particular events.

Getting the month as well as the year of specific events is helpful. One often sees the emergence of symptoms in one family member or a relationship after one or more shifts or changes in another part of the family. Having specific dates will highlight these nodal events in the emotional system. Often, they indicate how anxiety went up before the emergence of a symptom.

I would always ask people about critical turning points in their own lives, who was most affected, and the outcome of these turning points. Usually, they occurred around some significant family event, although people may not have connected their own "turning point" to the family event. When we think we have discovered such a connection, we should not rush to interpret this to people and say, "See how this is connected to that?" Let it be. We may just muse or wonder about it out aloud and whether there is any connection, but our job is not to convince or enlighten others.

5. RESEARCHING THE TOXIC ISSUES

Most families have issues and people they consider problematic and would rather not talk about for fear of upsetting someone. It can be money, death, divorce, wills, alcohol, gambling, womanizing, and bad sheep in the family. As people get more comfortable with us, we can begin to address these issues more specifically with family members. If we can begin to talk openly with people without either our or their getting jittery about it, we have begun to detoxify the issue. The purpose is not to talk them out of their beliefs or stances but just to develop a research approach to the issue. The research approach can help to lower people's level of anxiety, making them more comfortable talking about and exploring uncomfortable issues. Such an approach lets them know we are interested not in arguing the issues but rather in understanding their experience around the issues.

I mentioned that my mother had a brief separation from Mike and that she didn't move out because of his drinking. The issue turned out to be writing their wills. When I went down to help her move, I said to her, "You have done this a few times before. What is it like for you?" And then we began to talk about, among other things, why she was doing this move. I had assumed she had gotten fed up with his drinking, so I was surprised to hear the real reason. They wanted to do their wills differently, and Mom got really upset. I began to ask about the history of this upset.

It went back to her "wicked stepmother." Her father and stepmother, Mary, had a verbal agreement that whoever died first would leave all that they had to the other partner. Mary had asked for this. For some reason my grandfather had put the title of their house in Mary's name. He had also bought the house next door and done the same thing. It was assumed that this was also at Mary's request. The houses were paid for, and they were the total of what my grandfather owned.

Mary died first, and then it came out that, in her will, she left everything to her two nephews. One of the parents of these nephews was a sibling of hers, and both that sister and her husband had been killed in a car accident. The nephews were long grown and working, and the rest of the family couldn't see why she had done this. Grandpa lost everything with her death. The second house had provided the rental income that he lived on. This sealed the attitude for Mom and her siblings that Mary was a wicked woman.

This was the background to the upset with Mike. Mike had children from a previous marriage, and he and Mom had disagreed on how they would divide their money among all the children with their deaths. My questions helped Mom to think things through more clearly, and she and Mike eventually worked out an agreement. Mom moved back in.

In this one situation, the research stance was so successful at detoxifying an issue that I was able to move it further into the one-on-one relationship with my mother. Mike's alcohol cure did not take, and his drinking became worse than ever. All three of his adult kids became very concerned with him, and he got really angry at what he thought was their "interference." He told Mom he was going to write them out of his will entirely, and she said to him, "You will not." Her own family experience led to her firm stand on this. It wasn't long before his liver shut down, and he died in a gruesome way at home, bleeding to death. Mom was the executor of his will, and we had a family meeting where she read it and allocated the monies to his kids. She did well with this part, but she wasn't going to let his kids near any of Mike's personal belongings. She had taken on some of his anger at them.

When I got home the next day, I decided to write her a letter commending her on how well she handled everything. Then I thought it was time to try out the status of a more direct, one-on-one relationship. I told her that she had some experience with "wicked stepmothers" and that I feared she was edging in that direction with Mike's kids. She'd had a pretty good relationship with them until the critical time before his death. I said that I feared she was thinking with Mike's head rather than her own. It seemed reasonable to me that they should be able to go through his things and to claim anything of his they wanted. So I asked her to consider relenting on her position.

The letter got there fast. The day she got it, she called to tell me, in a warm and friendly way, that she wasn't going to become "a wicked step-mother" and that she had decided to let the kids deal with Mike's personal things. My belief was that we had gotten to a place in our relationship where we could say such things to each other without it becoming a major issue, or meddling, and that we could be a resource to each other's thinking. The research stance was a means for getting to this goal. I couldn't have gotten there without having first done that. In many cases, the direct relationship comments may not be appropriate, and it will take more time before they can be made. We have to play this by ear.

•

6. EXPLORING RELATIONSHIP CUTOFFS

As we visit as many people in our family as possible, including distant relatives, and report back on these visits to our immediate family, new information will emerge about these other relationships that immediate family members had "forgotten." There is often a reason that these relationships have drifted apart, and some sort of emotional cutoff has usually occurred. Other relationships are clearly intentional cutoffs and will involve stronger emotional intensity. In either case they represent unfinished business for the family, issues that may well affect us in unseen ways.

The main reason we usually fail to bridge the major cutoffs in our families is because we believe that some other member of the family that we are close to will be upset. They may see it in a triangular way as a betrayal of their own position and say, "You are going over to the enemy." So, in some cases, this can be difficult work and involves major deconstruction of the triangle.

Major cutoffs between formerly close members of a family don't usually happen overnight. They have a long history to them that may even go back to previous generations. They have a lot of emotional momentum. But after the cutoff has been bridged, people often wonder, "What was all the fuss about?"

In any case it is important to bridge the cutoffs by contacting all family members. Try to get their story on the family, not just about the issues around which the cutoff happened. Sometimes the cutoff has happened with people who were regarded as "crazy" and who may even have been institutionalized. Perhaps our parents wanted to protect us from such people. These people may have an important story to tell, so reach out to them. The same goes for all the other people who may have been considered criminals, deviates, or "bad characters" who disappeared from the family.

Part of what happens in cutoff is that the definition of family changes. Some family members have been excluded, and we are supposed to remain loyal to those triangular decisions. We need to realize that these cutoffs represent intense unresolved attachments in the family and that these excluded members are indeed family. They have a broader and different perspective to offer. Just remember the issue is not "who is right" or "who is telling the truth" or "does the story fit the facts?" What we learn will be aspects of the way the emotional process works in our family. We have to define family for ourselves.

If we are able to make progress on these six principles, we will begin to uncover most of the emotionally significant issues in our family. Uncovering them will help to set the stage and frame our own self-defining work in family, our process of defining or differentiating a self. As we learn to see how our emotional system functions and allow time for relationships to develop and issues to emerge, and as we continue to work at managing our own level of anxiety, we will be well launched on doing solid family of origin work.

8

THE RESEARCH STANCE

BECOMING A STUDENT OF YOUR FAMILY

All families, and every person in a family, develop their own explanatory story about who they are and how they got to be that way. Implicit in their stories is a sense that "we are 'this' kind of family, who do 'these' sort of things and not 'those.' And that is why I, because I accept or reject those things, do what I do." Going further, it can become "This is why I am the way I am. What would you expect a person like me to do when I have a family like that? How could I help being the way that I am?" We often fail to see how this simplistic cause-and-effect thinking about family locks us in and reduces our sense of self and freedom to act. By retaining the story we have of our family and of ourselves, we stay stuck in our lives. Our stories justify how we run our lives in relationships.

These family stories are not built by a rational novelist who is developing a plot with a specific direction and a particular outcome. They are subjectively built, mostly without awareness, based on feelings and experiences in the larger family. These experiences become gradually a part of a larger pattern within which the family develops certain themes or ways of looking at these experiences. Bowen theory helps us understand these subjective experiences by describing the more objective and observable processes by which they have been developed. It also offers a way to change our story more intentionally so that we have greater freedom of action and better emotional health.

It is a challenge if both parents are dead when we are ready to begin this work, but it does not make the work impossible. Are there relatives or good friends still around who can talk about them? Who was their best friend? Who did they talk with about their joys and their sorrows? Anyone who was a part of their same emotional field can help. Coworkers in their workplace might also be an option. But remember that these people also may feel on guard about why we are asking questions. They may want to preserve the memory of their family member or friend, so, just as with anyone else, the relationship has to be cultivated so that they can feel safe giving us more accurate information. Coming at them with a barrage of questions on first contact will probably not work.

Even when we think "everyone" in our family is dead, there are probably still relatives around that we haven't thought of or just haven't thought of as "family." The higher our level of motivation, the more likely we are to find relatives whom we may not have been aware of before. If we truly have no relatives left, Bowen theory suggests finding a person outside of our immediate daily life whom we dislike or find "difficult" and work on being a less reactive self while also better connecting with that person.

In the case of adoption, the family one grew up in is the most important, especially if the adoption happened early in life. However, if a person knew of being adopted early on and had begun to have a fantasy about the birth family and the story behind the adoption, then that can be worth exploring. The "fantasy family" will play a role in the emotional process of the adopted family. Usually, however, the more intense the desire to discover one's biological family, the more the real issue lies with the adoptive family and not the birth family. The fantasy may be about distancing from the adoptive family, from which differentiation still needs to occur.

GETTING THE FUNCTIONAL FACTS

A major part of family work is researching these family stories and themes to discover the emotional process by which they have developed. In this way we discover more clearly our own emotional context and clarify the decisions we need to make for growth. The primary way we go about doing this is by asking questions and listening to responses.

At a minimum, we want to find out dates of birth, marriage, divorce, and death for each person. We want to know family members' level of education and in what field. What occupation(s) did they pursue? How well did they do? What sort of family member were they? What chronic diseases did they have, and what were the dates of diagnosis and flare-ups? What hospitalizations did they have? How did they die? Generally, how did they do in life; what was their life course like?

In looking at the family diagram (discussed in chapter 7), ask the following questions: Where is the information spotty? What key data are missing, particularly for those members who are still living and accessible? What anxieties exist that have created this gap in information, and what anxieties may be encountered in contacting the people for information?

We want to better understand the functional facts of the family system. How do people actually move within the system? Rather than just listening to what people say they do, or did, what is it that they actually do? People can fool themselves. They may say they weren't upset about what someone did, but then they have distanced from that person. Believe the distancing rather than what they say. In our subjectivity, we are not always aware of how we function objectively. What did a person *do* in response to an event, rather than what did the person *say*? Who moves toward whom and away from whom, at what point and in what way? And what happens next?

As researchers we are interested in the what, when, where, how, and with whom type of questions, not the unending "why" questions related to motivation. Individual motivation is a complicated topic that no one really as yet understands. Many reasons are involved in the decisions we make. Our directions in life are multidetermined. At best, we can say that people are most often trying to feel safe and comfortable around their anxiety.

The biggest danger in doing family work is to think, "Now I know these people. I have them all figured out." Think about it. Who really knows you and how you function? We don't know ourselves all that well, so it is even less likely that we are truly known to others. It is a unique effort to try to understand the functional patterns of others rather than to try to evaluate their functioning or motivations.

Research will include identifying the major triangles in the family and how they function. What are the anxiety-inspiring issues or relationships that can stir them up? Who are the players? How do they typically play their part in the triangles? What is your own part in them? Do you ever initiate triangles yourself?

Bowen theory will keep you on track in this work. When you see the development of particular symptoms in a person or a relationship, consider what buildup of anxiety may have led to it: Symptoms may emerge in the physical, emotional, or social functioning of a key family member. Alcoholism, for example, would involve all three areas. They could also emerge as marital conflict or in the projection process focused on a particular child. Gather as much data as you can about the events that led up to the emergence of the symptom.

The theory is the underlying guide to our questions. We use the theory for our own personal understanding, not to teach anyone else anything about family. Our questions ought not to be implicit lessons on, for example, "Don't you see how you/we got this way?" This kind of approach is just part of the reactive process and will lead nowhere.

Family members are the teachers, and we are the learners, not the other way around. We don't take our specialized knowledge about family processes to them to teach them. Who they are—how they see the world, their lives, and their relationships and how they have acted within them—is our focus. Most of us have probably never learned much about the hopes and fears, beliefs, values, and goals of our family members. As we become more objective and less focused on insisting on our own story as the truth, then we can begin to take in their experience and see how it fits in the family system.

We may well find that as we ask our questions, people will begin to think more about their own experience in family and even become more skeptical about their own story. That is fine, but we are not promoting that for them. This is research we do only for ourselves, not to "publish." If they become curious and start asking their own questions, let them do so on their own.

THE ANXIETY OF BEING A RESEARCHER

We may resist asking the questions and doing significant research in our families because we don't want to have to change our stories. Our current stories provide us with a certain level of comfort even if they are "negative." At some level we may know that changing the story will mean changing ourselves. Our labels about "them," our family members, help to keep our world in place. Doing this research, which is full of unknowns, may be threatening to us. We are not sure we want to go into that new territory.

For me, challenging the theme of "I don't have a father" was very difficult to do. I had no sense of what it would mean for me, what would be required of me, and how I would want to handle it, if I allowed myself to think, "I do have a father." I hung onto the myth as long as I could. I knew that changing it would require a radical shift in my own sense of reality and way of being. I just didn't know in what way it would change. By the time I started to recognize that I did have a father and to follow up on what had become of him and try to make contact with him, he had been dead for two years. That was not the end of the story, but it had been slow in coming. The resistance lay in my own anxiety.

We need to ask ourselves: "Do we want to do this research? Do we want to suspend our judgments and assumptions and get clearer about how we function and what it is that we don't know?" To become a researcher in our family requires letting go of the anxiety that restricts growth and moving into the anxiety of positive growth, which goes into the unknown. We must be willing to go where the inquiry takes us and to change directions as new information emerges.

We have to reflect on whether there are things we haven't asked about and avenues that are opened to us that we have ignored rather than pursuing. What is going on with us, at this point? How did we manage to miss that comment or story? In what ways are we resisting doing the research? What do we think would happen if we went back to that missed comment? What is the anxiety about in us?

Or, are we in a triangle we don't see or don't want to challenge in our own thinking? Someone may make a comment about someone else in the family toward whom we have either a positive or a negative stance. If the comment goes against our stance, then we may just avoid the topic rather than exploring how the person reached that stance. This is assuming we can avoid stating our position outright. Can we let go of our own triangular convictions to hear someone else's view of "the facts"? We are not doing a good job as a researcher if we can't step out of our own triangular positions long enough to hear someone else's different experience of a relationship and explore it with interest. Making this reach may be a significant change for the relationship.

REENTRY, RESEARCH, AND REPOSITIONING

Assuming the research stance is the best way to reenter our family, we have to go back to our family with lots of questions. We have to go with the idea that we really don't know these people and how we all got to be the way we are. In spite of all the years we spent with them, we are now going to get to know them from an adult point of view, using a helpful way of understanding family processes. We don't teach them about family systems theory; we just use it as a guide in asking our questions. Beyond knowing them in their family role as dad or mom or sister or brother, we want to know them as people who have their own story. We go back to them with a respect for their story and to hear how they have made sense of what has happened to them in life.

The process isn't about getting buddy-buddy with them or having a love-in. It isn't about getting closer and warmer and having a big group hug. We can do that, but that is not the point of the work. Nor is it about forgiving them or telling them off or finally confronting them with what they did to us. When people work just at trying to discover, with a more objective attitude, how things got the way they are for each person in the family, the need for all of those things begins to disappear.

Interesting things may emerge from learning the family history and hearing the stories, but that is not the ultimate goal. The process serves as a safer way for us and other people to manage our reentry into the family in a new way. As we do the research, we are actively changing our positions and functioning in the triangles within the family system. Going to family members with curiosity and interest rather than with all of our old feelings about them and without seeking to reconfirm what we have always known and believed about them is a part of redefining ourselves in the family.

By using what the theory tells us about family functioning, we can discover what we have never thought to look at or ask before. Where are the gaps and holes in the story? What connections have we never before seen? What undiscovered processes have been at work? What succession of events took place that provides a thread that no one has ever noticed before? Each answer to every question we ask should suggest five more questions. Then we will begin to get new information and hear about things we have never considered.

Researchers are curious. Keep a notebook of the questions you want to ask each family member. If you run out of questions, you are probably reactively caught in some emotional issue and have taken a position in a triangle. Make sure you are asking real questions that ask for information. Many questions people ask are actually disguised statements and interpretations. If you begin a question with some version of "Don't you think . . . ?" then you are not really asking a question. You are wondering if the person agrees with your position or not. The information you are asking for is limited to your own perceptions. Leading questions do not evoke much information about the person you are talking with.

A question that begins with "Why . . ." is not likely to tell you much about family process. It often gets a defensive response. Human motivation is very complicated and highly subjective. Questions that begin with "who," "what," "where," "when," "how," and "with whom" will tell you more objectively about how the family emotional process functions. It may also help to test the conclusions you are drawing by asking "Do you mean . . . ?" questions.

RESEARCH AND REACTION

As mentioned earlier, people may react differently to our new way of being with them. They may well be initially suspicious, guarded, and slow to respond. Or they may say, "What are you up to? Why all of these questions all of a sudden?" It is just fine to say something like, "You know I have never thought much about your life before I was born and what experiences you have had in life. I have been pretty self-centered. I'd just like to get to know you better. Would you help me do that?"

If they are still suspicious, then we have to go slower and do everything we can to develop a more positive relationship. Give them sincere compliments, and tell them things that we think they do well. But don't make up stuff—everybody does something well. Let them know we see it, for example, by asking, "And by the way, how did you learn to do that so well?" Slowly they will begin to warm to our questions if they see that they are not threatened and that they don't have to be automatically defensive. People do like to talk about themselves and their lives, once they feel safe. This helps account for the popularity of therapy.

It's best not to ask any questions about family members' picture of us or our growing up. That could be dangerous territory for them. They may volunteer things about us and our early days, but keep the focus on them. This part of the research effort is not about us. Remember Bette Midler's famous self-centered line in the film *Beaches*, "Well, that's enough talking about me. Let's talk about you. What do *you* think of me?" This is what you want to avoid.

In the end we have to demonstrate that we are not going to "do" something with the information or that we are not out to "prove a point" or "build a case" or develop some "interpretation" of them. We just keep our focus on them and their experience of relationships, not ours. As we succeed at this, they will quickly relax and become more open. And they will start telling us things we didn't even ask about. Maybe they have never told anyone these things before. Be very respectful of this material.

RESEARCH AND THE ONE-ON-ONE RELATIONSHIP

Don't expect this interest to become a two-way street. If family members ask what we think about certain subjects or experiences in the family, be careful. They are not asking their questions in the same spirit, usually, that we are. Their questions are usually more triangular, wondering, "Whose side are you on in this story?" Unless we are at the point of making "I" statements, something that normally comes later in the process, we need to be careful. The time will come when we can respond directly and openly; that is our goal. But the atmosphere may not yet exist so that we can do this. It took me about two years to get to this point.

We do need to take responsibility for how we are present in the family. What is our own part in the family emotional process? What is our part in stirring up the difficulties in the family? What do we know about our own reactivity, and how do others experience it? What do they do with it? And what do we do with their reactions to our reactions? How do others see us? Do we see how they may think we are problematic? Can we be comfortable with their having that perception and not need to straighten them out? These are not questions we ask them. We attempt to deduce the answers as we watch ourselves functioning in the system.

Genuinely taking on the research stance will help us release some of our own reactivity, but we still need to be aware of our impulses to react.

Can we learn to predict what our part in the family process would typically be and how that affects the overall process? Learning to predict what happens next is one of the useful results of doing good research.

But the goal of this work is to get to the point where everyone in the family can openly and relatively comfortably say what they think, feel, or do about any subject, including our own behavior, and not have it become an occasion for a blowup or create a lot of reactivity. When people can talk more calmly about important issues and relationships, with different opinions expressed, then real progress has been made in the family. It just takes a lot of time for most of us. Remember how long it took for things to get to the way they are—generations. We won't overcome that generational momentum quickly. And some, perhaps most, relationships just will never get there. This has to be accepted as well. But any movement in this direction, in any relationship, will be a real plus.

Learning to adopt the research stance is one of the biggest shifts we can make in our family work. It is also a useful way to function in our church. We can just as easily assume we know what is going on with people there: what motivates them and what their "problems" are, and how this will keep things stuck as a result. We need to question our own assumptions about what is "true" and pay more attention to what we don't know rather than what we do know. As soon as we think we have people figured out, we usually start trying to change them, which they will naturally resist, and we will be at odds. The research stance provides a new kind of relationship with church members.

9

DEFINING A SELF AND TRIANGLES

DIFFERENTIATION AND TRIANGLES

Differentiating a self within our family is nearly impossible without addressing triangles. Triangles are the basic molecules of emotional systems. Organized around a family's emotional sensitivities, they are always present, even when dormant. They become active as anxiety builds in the system. They are a way people in systems attempt to get a better level of emotional safety. Over time they can become automatically repetitive or fixed, and then family patterns become predictable.

Understanding triangles as the major way people manage emotional intensity in relationships is essential to doing family of origin work. The shifting drama of two insiders and one outsider is as old as human beings and can be observed in other forms of life. We are all just trying to find a more comfortable and less anxious position in relationships. The higher the anxiety, the more likely that the triangular processes will emerge and that other, interlocking triangles will become active. For example, people take sides on issues in the family. We are asked, or we ask others, to be on a side. We may pull in people outside the family to help. Pastors, for example, are often pulled into the family triangles of church members.

Here is an example. If your mother continues to think that you agree with her about your father, you won't be able to get closer to your father. Her communications to him about you will disincline him to you. She may directly say to him, "And Bill agrees with me that you are wrong." Or she may find some way to intimate that you and she are on the same side, that you are in "her camp." Or, if your father tells your mother that you agree with him that she is "crazy," then your mother will not open up to you. You have to find a way to communicate to them both that you are your own person and only in your "own camp." You won't be able to do this if you are caught up in the content of who is right or wrong in their disagreements.

As we grow up and become mature adults, we define a self within our family automatically, without any knowledge of Bowen theory or triangles. It is simply the way we develop; it is a normal part of maturation. I defined myself in the triangle with my mother and the church without even knowing what I was about. She was generally negative about the church, and I was only dimly aware of that because she never made an issue of it. Being a pastor was not something she would have wanted for me, but she kept that to herself. Even though it represented a kind of personal threat for her and was something she was initially anxious about, she came to terms with my decision without any discussion between us on the topic. Since I believed I was free to choose my direction in life, I decided that my faith was important to me and that I wanted to represent it in the world. She had fostered this basic belief in my freedom to make my own choices. I didn't even think about her position in making my decision, but the decision was a repositioning within that triangle before I knew anything about the theory.

As we grow up, most of us make many such decisions about self, our directions in life, and our relationships, which are not strongly resisted by our family. The more mature the family, the less difficulty there exists with the self-definition of each person in it. Each person is free to move ahead in life as he or she sees fit. But every family has some sensitivities, some areas of anxiety, that become an inhibitory experience for the growing individuals. Having respected these sensitive areas, they carry these unresolved emotional issues into adult life and continue to function out of them, with and often without awareness.

Perhaps a nuclear family has an issue about the dating habits of the teenage daughter. Dad quietly supports his daughter's position that she should be able to stay out later, and the mother is the "ogre" who is "unjustly" restricting her. Dad allows the battle to go on between mother and daughter, and he may take secret delight in watching the daughter sock it to the mother. But he is not really as close to his daughter as it appears, and he is just using his daughter in his undeclared disagreement with his wife. Husband and wife both fail to sort out their parenting policy (and other differences), and the daughter gets focused on. This is a standard triangle brought into counseling.

The mother may go to her pastor and make a moral case for the correctness of her position. The pastor may either agree or disagree with her position and then feel trapped. The pastor is caught in the content of what "should" be done, rather than paying attention to the family process. The only way to get out of the triangle, however, is to take interest in something different from the parents. How did they manage to create this difference? What does it take to maintain it? What would happen if someone relented? How would that happen? What would be the cost? Is there a way for them both to have their own positions as they parent, without it being a battle? When do they most disagree? What seems to be at stake at those times? What is the background to that? The questions can go on forever, but the pastor is asking the parents to think more about what they bring to this difference.

SOME INDICATORS OF TRIANGLES

1. Pursuit and Distance.

Patterns of pursuit and distance are a part of the predictable process that indicates a triangle is at work. As anxiety increases, people will begin to move toward and away from one another, and then either party may move toward others to enlist their help or succor. These patterned ways of moving reveal that a triangle exists.

2. Side Taking.

It is not unusual for a person, growing up, to take one side in the parental triangle, to always be on the mother's or father's side in their struggles. One parent is seen as the persecutor of the other, who is seen as a victim. The side taking can be openly declared or just a silent, emotionally felt position, revealed in nothing more than body posture and a look of the eyes. If one or both parents attempt to enlist the child into taking sides, it becomes even more intense. This fixed pattern can then be carried into our professional life as pastors. We will frequently see replications of the triangle in various relationships, and we will often act out our old pattern of taking sides.

3. Overfunctioning/Underfunctioning.

Another indicator of triangles is overfunctioning and underfunctioning patterns. Overfunctioning is a way of pursuing by focusing on the "needs" of the other. Overfunctioners can avoid personal anxiety and a sense of inadequacy—which stems from something the overfunctioners once could do nothing about—by focusing on doing for others. Now, to keep that old feeling at bay, they have to keep doing for people they think can't do for themselves, although, in most cases, they could if challenged. Letting the overfunctioner take charge allays the underfunctioner's anxiety as well.

For example, a younger brother could "crumble" under his father's demands, sending an "I can't do it" message. If the father's demands continued, then an older brother might step in and challenge the father to protect his younger brother. If the younger brother were to become a pastor, he might find a church leader who would step in and cover for him (assuming he was otherwise well-liked) whenever he began to feel overwhelmed by the demands of work. His dependency would allow the leader to play out his family drama as well. The pastor would just be seen as "hopeless" around certain situations, and he would be allowed to get off the hook. But the overfunctioner most likely would not complain.

If the older brother were to become a pastor, then he might be looking for "younger brothers" to rescue from someone in the church who is perceived as "too demanding." Or, conceivably, he could step into his father's shoes and begin to be the demanding parent in the church, and others would be the rescuers of whomever became the substitute younger brother. In this way whatever triangular patterns were established at home with the family can easily become a regular repetitive drama for pastors in the church.

WORKING ON TYPICAL FAMILY TRIANGLES

Among all of the possible triangles a family can have, one in particular usually appears to be the problem. However, if that one quiets down for some reason, others will emerge, given enough anxiety. There will always be surprises around triangles in doing our work. Wherever differentiation is lacking, there will be triangles. The relationship with the least amount of differentiation in it will usually be the most problematic.

Assuming the research stance, we can gradually become more objective around the functioning of these triangles. Without openly declaring to the other participants, "I don't do triangles. That is wrong," we can gradually become more neutral within them. When the mother wants to talk to us about the father and "his problems" (and assuming we have already tried saying, "I think you should talk with Dad about this rather than me"), we can lightly say something like, "Mom, it is wonderful how concerned you are about Dad. He should know how loving you are. But then if he knew, what else could you do with your love? This seems to be your calling in life. I hope he appreciates it." And to the dad you could say something like, "Dad, do you know why your wife keeps telling me about her difficulties with you? She says you are [whatever content may apply]."

Comments like these cannot sound cruel or sarcastic. This would be evidence that we are still caught in the emotionality. There has to be a way we can say them genuinely, in a calm and neutral way. The point is to put the anxiety back into the relationship, where it belongs, not with us as the third person who can do nothing about the relationship between the other two. This last point can't be said straight out to the other members of the triangle. What we need to communicate is our neutrality on the issues between the two of them and that we can't be counted on to do anything to take on the mother's or father's anxiety or join in on either side of the issue.

I took a somewhat different tack with my mother, who would regularly complain about her husband, Mike, to me. Eventually, I decided that every time she told me something negative about him, I would ask her about how she managed herself with the behavior. For example, if he did "this," then what did she do with it? How did she decide to do that? Had she ever tried any other ways of doing it? How successful did she think she was? Asking her many questions like this communicated that I couldn't change anything between the two of them and that the main issue was "What was she going to do about her problem?" I never said that to her straight out or said anything directly about the triangle. I communicated my interest in "her" problem, not what she thought of as Mike's problems. My questions let her know that I thought it was between them. I was not advocating any particular behavior on her part, but eventually she stopped complaining and started acting differently with him. Over just a few visits with my asking these kinds of questions, she was better defining herself with him and being less reactive to him.

In detriangling we want to respond to the content of a triangular communication by addressing the process or the emotional context. We have to be aware of the process to make an effective response. Differentiation is about stepping out of this emotional process and our usual functional position within it. For example, when negative messages start coming at us from the mother or father, it may well be about the emotional process in the family or about their own anxiety and how they think we could make it better for them. Keeping this in mind may make it easier to be neutral and respond effectively.

Getting beyond our reactivity into a more neutral position—not what we specifically do or say—is the essential part. If we don't have the neutrality, what we do or say won't communicate anyway. As long as we are reactive, people in the system will know it and use it. The emotional pressure will only increase. Successful detriangling may create a short-term upset with people, causing such accusations as "You are so selfish; you don't care what happens and won't help me." But in the long run, all parties will appreciate our move toward neutrality. The key is calming our own anxiety, being less reactive, becoming truly neutral in how things play out, and staying well connected with everyone in the triangle.

Usually, the mother is involved in the most important family triangles because family emotional processes tend to funnel through mothers. For most of us, our relationship with her is the most intense one in the family, the one around which we can feel most anxious. Being vulnerable to her anxiety is a natural part of the developmental process of growing up. Initially, it is a good thing and serves as a key to survival for most animals. When mother bear grunts in a particular way, the cubs immediately run up the nearest tree. However, this sensitivity to mother's anxiety is usually the last thing we let go of as we mature. Many of us never really lose it.

I do not mean that the mother is the focus of blame here or the cause of these triangles. She is just the central player in the larger family process only because of her essential role. If the father had played that role in the family emotional process, then he would be the focal point of anxiety. Usually, fathers have taken the outside position to the mother's and the children's closer position, and that is part of the larger process. Is there a way that father and mother can be the closer twosome? They don't really have to be in agreement or have a united front, but can they become more of a resource to the thinking of the other as they each do their own parenting?

When I went home for visits, I didn't want to spend all my time with Mother because I wanted to see old friends. This was a very powerful triangle for me. It was somehow "disloyal" to my mother to want to do this on my rare visits home. It was as if she deserved all of my time when I was in town. It is interesting how this was a repetition of the triangle my mother felt with her stepmother. She had no sense that she was repeating an old drama, and I never pointed it out to her. So just as she might have done with her mother, either I didn't let her know I was in town (Los Angeles is a big city), or, more often, I just stayed away. I was not happy with either option. In doing my family work, I decided I had to deal with this.

Finally, I began making visits to friends on my visits home. I didn't make a big deal of it or have a fight with her about it. I just did it. She was not happy. Each time I would leave the house to visit someone, she would be sad and say something like, "Do you *have* to?" I felt this powerfully but said, "No, but I *want* to." I told her that I was glad that she wanted to see me and that I wanted to see her too, but that I also wanted to see some friends. Without making a point about it or blaming her for my uneasiness, I stayed nonreactively firm with my decision and did not relent. We both got over the hump, and it made visiting her much easier and more frequent. My mother adjusted to my position. With each visit Mom would say, "When can I count on seeing you?" That was a good way to do it. This is a small, undramatic example, but it involved powerful feelings that were difficult for me to deal with. But in being more of my own self with her on this issue, I also felt able to be closer to her when I was there with her.

In these tough areas of growth, we want our parents, for example, to validate our decisions and to cooperate with them. But that is not how it works. In these areas where becoming a self creates anxiety for them (as well as for us), we can't count on cooperation and may instead experience outright struggles against our self-definition. This nearly always involves triangles and anxiety. It stimulates an underlying fear or sense of loss, regret, or vulnerability in our parents. These are all part of their unresolved issues, and so they resist our differentiating moves. And we comply, or rebel, or argue and fight, or distance out of our own anxious, reactive response. A sibling (or other relative) may get involved in the triangle at this point and say, "Why are you doing this to Mom (or Dad)? Stop it."

The issue for us is whether we can nonreactively continue with what makes sense to us to do and still stay connected with them, not needing to distance in order to be a self. Our distancing is the way we try to lower our anxiety and make it safe or more comfortable for us, but it only creates more reactivity in the system and resolves nothing. Can we stay positively connected with our parents, while they are experiencing their fears and losses and critically focusing on us, without having their emotionality run our lives? And without needing them to say, "You do as you want, dear"?

Getting one-on-one relationships established in the family is nearly impossible without addressing the triangles. Getting close to each person can be disturbing to the established triangular relationships. Usually, for example, getting closer to our father won't happen until we have achieved a level of neutrality on his and our relationship with our mother. This is often one of the toughest knots to sort through, but it normally precedes being able to do anything with other triangles in the family. For example, getting better connected with a sibling may require first dealing with the parental triangle. Traditionally, siblings have taken sides in the parental triangle and tend to define their relationship with one another around these positions. True neutrality is the only way out of this.

Another good triangle to work on is our mother and our maternal grandmother. Remember that this is an intense one for the mother. Her siblings, our aunts and uncles, will also be in on this. Getting close to any of them may stir some reactivity with the mother. But as we go up to previous generations, we are able to become more objective about our own. How did each one of them grow up, and what emotional challenges did each face in the process? Just realizing that our mother or father had parental struggles to sort through and whether or how well they did this really helps. We can then see the nature of some of the emotional intensity that comes at us and put it in a clearer, less personalized perspective.

Counselors regularly get caught in triangles with their counselees. The counselees present some "awful" story about their family or a family member, and the counselor has no systemic way to view the story and sides with the clients. The clients then feel supported and justified in their reactions, enjoying the supportive empathy of their counselor, but change does not happen. I can't say how often I have had people to whom this happened in counseling before they came to me. The counselors, often psychiatrists, will diagnose various members of a family, sight unseen, based on stories told by the client. These diagnoses are taken back into the system, causing further uproar.

This was part of an issue in one workgroup I consulted with. The group had divided into two camps, for and against the director. Everyone in the group knew about the conflict between the director and one of his workers. That worker had filed grievances against the director through the union, and a significant reaction was happening. Several factors were contributing to this situation, but one significant ingredient was the director's own therapist, a psychologist, who had labeled the problematic worker as a "borderline personality" and had told the director that things could never get better and that the only option was to fire the worker.

As a part of the consultation, I did some family of origin work with the director. As a result, he began to get a new perspective on the parallel problems with his family and with the staff group. The director began a repositioning process in both emotional systems and began functioning differently. At this point I got a phone call from the psychologist telling me that I didn't know what I was getting into, that it was absolutely clear that the staff member was a borderline personality and things would not improve. Somewhat taken aback, I said that I didn't realize that he had ever met the staff member involved, implying that he had diagnosed someone he had never met. The psychologist said that was true, but still there was no question about the diagnoses. I thanked him for letting me know his thinking and proceeded with the work.

The director continued to work at repositioning, and he did an excellent job. The union issue just fizzled out. Eventually, the problematic staff person resigned, without any pressure from the director, in order "to reconsider future career directions." The staff divisions ceased. The members of the staff put their full energy into their work mission that we had done some work in clarifying. The diagnoses of the psychologist could well have been correct, but still it was not impossible to sort things out. Labeling and taking sides in the triangle were not the way to do it, however, and luckily the union had no energy for the effort either. If they had had a political agenda of their own in the triangle, we might not have sorted it out.

Many pastors still consider detriangling to be some kind of tricky therapeutic technique for doing things to families rather than clearly seeing triangles as a normal, basic building block of systems and under-standing that developing neutrality within these triangles is essential to differentiating a self. They think of the process as doing things to others rather than managing self differently, in a more neutral fashion, within the emotional system.

To successfully work at the process of differentiation, we have to be aware of the triangles in our family life and the emotional process of which they are a part. We also have to see our part in that process. Fail-ure to do this is how the effort is most often thwarted. We have to think: Where are the triangles in my family? What is the anxiety that gets them started, and what is the typical process? What are the patterns of pursuit and distance? Who ends up being "it," the person on whom the anxiety has landed and become symptomatic? Who are the other players? How am I involved? What would it look like for me to be neutral in all of this? What will it take for me to do this and push the anxiety back to where it belongs or at least not to take it on? How will I maintain my position when the pressure to go back to my old way of functioning increases?

The pressure to go back to the old way of functioning will normally be intense. This is the critical point in detriangling work. If we relent, things won't change. If we get reactive and blame others for this or tell them in some way, "Help me out here; I am trying to do something good for the family!" we have missed the point. We have to get to that neutral point, not to get reactive and not to take on the anxiety. We need to be able to make a comment about the situation that is not sarcastic or blam-ing, one that says to the other, in effect, "I am not taking on this anxiety; what are you going to do with it now?" When we succeed at this process and are truly neutral, we can get on with building a one-on-one rela-tionship with the people involved—but not until then.

10

SAM'S EXAMPLE

Sam was a thirty-eight-year-old, divorced pastor from a "nonobservant" Jewish family. He had converted to Christianity in college after having positive contact with a university chaplain and several Christian friends. Shortly after his conversion he decided he wanted to go to seminary to learn more about his new faith and to see if he wanted to be a pastor. Surprisingly, his family accepted this position for the most part, except his older sister, who found it to be "just one more thing to be critical of" about him. They were used to his doing unusual things, and though this went over the top a bit, they thought it was "typical" of the kind of thing he would do. Here is his family diagram.

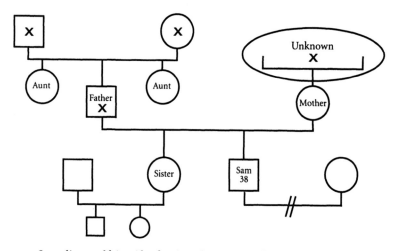

Sam divorced his wife after just three years of marriage. Then he had a succession of girlfriends, but he dropped each one. His complaint about his current girlfriend was basically the same one he had about the others; like them, she just wasn't "loving enough." She wasn't interested and caring and attentive to him the way he thought she should be. But he did still believe there was a woman out there who could give him what he was looking for, if he couldn't "shape up" the current girlfriend.

Sam was known as a sensitive, caring pastor. People responded well to both his intelligent, thoughtful sermons and his pastoral style. He said he was an "adequate" administrator, though he left as much as he could to others. He was often developing some new program or some special project for worship or education. He thought of himself as "a creative type."

Sam came to me for supervision of the counseling work he did in his church. In his individually focused model of counseling, he strongly supported his parishioners. He thought this was his best attribute as a counselor. His basic counseling belief seemed to be that people needed a "corrective loving experience" after failing to get this in their families. If they could just experience his acceptance of all of their feelings as well as his interest in, support, and love for them, then they could do well in their lives and make good decisions. He did well in pursuing this goal.

People came eagerly to counseling sessions with him and were very appreciative of his care. He reported them as saying things like, "I wish you could have been my father." And some of them, with his support, began to complain to or confront their parents with their "lack of love." His hope was that the parents would "shape up" and come forth with the wanted "love." However, he would gradually come to believe, with his parishioners, that they would never be able to offer what the person "needed."

Sam was struggling with spending too much time doing counseling in his church and neglecting other pastoral duties, and his board was beginning to question him about this. While they recognized that he was "good" at this kind of pastoring, they thought he needed to limit the time he devoted to it. He agreed with them on this, but he had difficulty saying "no" to people who wanted counseling with him.

Sam found his parishioners' intense attachment to him gratifying in that it meant he was accomplishing his goal. But this was also problematic. He noticed that, despite their appreciation of his love and support, they didn't seem to be getting better no matter how long he worked with them or how supportive he was. If anything, they were getting worse in terms of their daily functioning and would have a seemingly unending list of problems to present to him. He came to me thinking he needed some "new techniques" for getting them to change and to depend less on him. He had heard about "family systems stuff" and thought he would "try" that.

I told him I wanted him to do some reading in family systems theory in preparation for how I would supervise him. He readily agreed to this. Early on he tried to change the supervision with me into personal counseling work with a triangular focus on his girlfriend(s) and what "their problems" were. I simply said up front that I wouldn't talk with him about his present romantic relationships, but that if he were open to exploring more in his family of origin, I would be willing to make that a part of the supervision. He reluctantly agreed to this but said his family was "hopeless."

His father had been dead for years, but even when he was alive and before Sam had become a pastor, Sam had accused both parents of being inadequate and unloving. His training in counseling in a feeling-focused, individual model had reinforced this and given him additional intellectual support for his belief. He had undergone personal therapy with several therapists who had joined in a triangle with him around his parents, supported his beliefs about their inadequacy, and helped him further express his feelings about this loss of love and support.

His mother and sister lived in the town where he was working. His contacts with his mother would often gravitate to a debate about her mothering. When he was with his sister, she would defend his mother over these attacks and would counterattack him on his "erratic" life and some of his personal habits.

In her relationship with her son, Sam's mother was highly defensive and could equally attack him, telling him in response to his accusations that he had been "a very difficult child" and was "not easy to love." She could provide examples of his bad behavior. She said that if he had been as "good" as his older sister, then all would be fine in the relationship. Sam would openly blame his mother for his difficulties with women and for not being able to find the love he "needed." This unending battle had been going on for years. He said in recent years all he had been trying to get from his mother was an "admission" that she had not been a good mother.

I worked with him on developing a more neutral research stance both in his counseling and with his family. I did this primarily by demonstrating it in the work I did with him. As it turned out, he didn't really know much about his extended family on his mother's side because they were all victims of the Holocaust. She was a survivor. He said that he had not asked her much at all about her losses and experiences because they would be "too painful" for his mother to talk about.

I asked him what would happen if he began to ask his mother about her family. He said this would immediately lead them into talking about the death camps, which would be "too sad for Mother" and cause her to cry. He had not thought that this might be a painful topic for him. Then I asked, "If she were willing to talk about it, what would be so awful if your mom would cry? What would it be like for you?" He immediately felt his own sadness and said, "Then I would feel sad and cry." Then I asked, "What would be so awful about you and your mother being sad and crying together?" In all of his feeling-focused therapy he had never thought about this before. He said, "I see your point. I guess it wouldn't be awful. Just very uncomfortable." As I saw it, he and his therapists had colluded to avoid this painful topic of loss. He was much more comfortable being angry with his mother than sitting with her in her sadness.

I asked Sam to sit down with his mother and to draw a family diagram with her. It was moving for me when I saw the diagram he brought in, with all of the crossed-out people, of all ages, who had died in the concentration camps. He was able to ask his mother many questions about her family and the memories and stories she had received from an aunt and uncle who had also escaped.

Of course, they both cried many times as they talked. But neither one let the pain of all that loss keep them from talking. As Sam reported back what he was learning from his mother, I suggested further questions he might pursue with the goal of getting him to be more objective about family and less feeling-focused. He was learning to be comfortable with his ignorance, after so many years of having his mother "all figured out." He was surprised that his mother was actually eager to talk with him about all of these things and was not at all inhibited by her unhappy feelings. In fact, she was grateful for his interest. When he asked her what had kept her from telling him these stories over the years, she said that she knew he was "a sensitive boy" who was easily upset and that they would cause him pain. She didn't want to burden him with all of that.

As he asked his mother more and more questions about her life and also about his father's life and family, the relationship between them began to change. Not once, for nearly six months, did they fight over or even talk about their own relationship over the years. Sam kept his focus entirely on his mother's and father's family experience. He was able to keep his own reactivity in check, and this reactivity gradually diminished. He also had a couple of aunts still alive on his father's side he could talk with, and he was able to talk with his sister in a new way. He showed interest in her experience of life and family over the years rather than trying to convince her of the validity of his. They established a good, new relationship that he found much more satisfying.

Sam became genuinely interested in his mother as a person. He began to see her as more than just his mother. He said it was the "most peaceful" time in their entire relationship. Then, one day, they were out for lunch, talking about family, and his mother said to him out of the blue, "and that's why I have never been an adequate loving mother for you." This was the "admission" he had been trying to force from her for years, and it just came freely. Sam later said to me, "You know, Ron, I heard those words of confession, and they just went right by me. I almost missed it actually. I didn't comment on it. It just didn't seem important to me anymore."

Sam no longer needed to hear his mother's confession because he had begun to develop such a different kind of relationship with her and had begun to redefine his own experience and think of himself differently. The thing that he had once thought would make all the difference with her was just not important anymore. His feelings had changed. He said he now saw her strengths, her courage, her capabilities, and the ways that she had been an adequate, loving parent. He said, "Mostly I feel gratitude now for having her as a mother."

Of course, Sam's work with his parishioners and his overall pastoral work were also changing. It was not easy for him to change his previous counseling beliefs, and he would keep sliding into them and then catching himself. I suggested that it was difficult to become a "novice" again after feeling comfortable and proficient in his old approach. He agreed and added that learning to "think systems" was such a different way to function. In addition, he felt the anxiety of not really knowing what his counseling work would be like if he gave up the old ways.

Subjectively, Sam felt himself being less involved and more distant from counselees. But he said it was "a good kind of distance; like I can see them better, more in context." He had once thought that his relationships with these people were the "most real" relationships he had. Now he began to see that they weren't "real" at all, in that they were one-sided since his counselees didn't know him. His view of the nature of the counseling relationship underwent a significant shift.

He initially felt some loss of the intense closeness he had felt with them, and he wasn't quite sure how to function. The people he had worked with the longest felt this change happening and would try to pull him back into the intensity. But he mostly stayed on course, relying on the theory as much as he could and attempting to be a researcher. Then he eventually decided that he didn't "need that kind of closeness" and that the dependency it fostered in his clients hadn't been good for them. He got it when I told him that Ed Friedman had once said, "Therapists are people who *need* twenty hours of therapy a week."

Sam began to take responsibility for his own part in the family emotional process and to reposition himself within it. He began to understand his own dependency in the family and how he was hooked on trying to get "loving support." It was like an addiction for him in that he could never get enough. He became much more realistic about the presence of love already in his life. He found his theology was changing as well. Of course, there was more work to be done, but he had turned a corner and was functioning differently.

One shift that happened was that his mother began to complain to him about his sister. In the past she had always complained to his sister about him. With the shift in his relationship to his mother, his sister had felt freer to spend more time with her family and leave their mom to him. He understood that it was just a shift in the triangle as to who the two insiders were, with no real change in the triangle itself. He began to see that his mother had a lot of understandable anxiety about being alone and that complaints, and even their fights, were a way to keep a kind of intense, distant connection without facing the vulnerability of her aloneness.

He ignored the complaints about his sister. Each time his mother complained, he asked her more questions about being a parent, particularly about what it was like after her husband died. He used the word *alone* a lot and asked how, as a younger parent, she had prepared for the day when her children would be more independent of her, living their own lives. He would observe that it must be hard spending so many years "being a loving and concerned and involved parent" and then not having that job any more. He said he worried about whether he could do it when he became a parent and asked her, "How did you manage to do it?" The shift in his own position had allowed him to ask these types of questions.

Gradually, his mother began spending more time with her friends and got into more social activities. Both he and his sister were spending more time in their own relationships and less time with their mom, with no complaints coming from her. In fact, she was often "too busy" to see them. Returning to the triangle, when Sam was with his sister, he said, "Mother has been telling me 'this and this' about you. I don't know why she is telling me rather than you. Do you?"

About a year after our interaction ended, I attended Sam's wedding. He said it was the best relationship with a woman he had ever had, which he attributed primarily to a change in his own understanding of relationships and in his expectations, rather than to "finally finding the right woman." He saw how he had been trying to redo his old, unresolved family attachment in his relationship with a woman as well as in his pastoral work. He had thought that the girlfriend and the work would help him overcome the disappointments he had felt in his family of origin. Previously, he had been changing women and considering a church move as a solution to his inner feelings of emptiness.

Sam now had a much better sense of how he had functioned in all of his emotional systems. He saw not only how family systems theory enlightened his family and emotional life but also how it worked in his church. He found its role "revolutionary" and became a serious student of the theory. It was now much easier for him to discover the emotional process around issues in his church, and he could address them more appropriately. He paid much more attention to the family life of his parishioners and could better see the frame of reference, values, and life goals they had created out of their family experiences.

Sam said that he now had "clear and realistic directions" for his own personal growth and the long-term development of differentiating a self in his various emotional systems. He wanted to learn to see "beyond the symptoms," to fully let go of his old beliefs about love, and to be patient with how much time change took. His connection with his church members was better than when he was so feeling-focused, and they noticed a "significant change" in him. He managed not to rush in and "teach" them all about it but just remained "curious" about what they noticed. Then he would bring that curiosity back to them and their own lives.

Sam experienced a deep, personal change as a result of doing this work in his family. Old feelings had resolved and seemingly "melted away." He said this was much more profound and meaningful than all of his previous therapies. He no longer saw the expression of feelings and the unending talking about relationships that he had been devoted to as the way to function. He brought his focus back to himself and to his own functioning. He remained only curious and ignorant about the functioning of others, asking them to teach him about themselves. As each relationship developed and matured, he could say things directly to others when it was required and then leave it for them to consider. He no longer needed to "convince" anyone that he was correct.

PART THREE

THE PASTOR AS COACH

11

MINISTRY AS COACHING

Doing our own family of origin work is the primary way we grow and become more emotionally mature and healthier persons. But as John Donne said, our lives are not "complete and entire" of themselves. Especially as pastors, we are closely connected to a community of people in which their health and ours are intertwined. As we grow and develop emotionally, so will they. We may fulfill our ministry to some of them by being their coach in their own family work.

Part three of this book is about how we may begin to introduce directly the concepts of family of origin work with our parishioners. In my book *Creating a Healthier Church*, I spoke about how to use family systems theory thinking in the larger framework of our congregational life. Here I will address a more focused and specific use of the theory in our ministry to individual members and their families. Teaching the concepts of family of origin work and coaching others in the work are further ways to develop our own health as pastors.

Learning to relate family systems theory in the ministry to our church members and to guide them in the process of beginning to differentiate a self within their own families will lead to healthier lives for us all. The community will grow and mature as well as the individual members.

THE PASTOR AS COACH

Even though he was a professor of psychiatry, Murray Bowen preferred to think of his kind of psychotherapy as "coaching" rather than therapy. He didn't like the implications of "a medical doctor diagnosing and treating sick patients" for his approach to therapy. He saw himself as having the same challenges to emotional growth and health as did his patients and felt that "we are all in it together." He was an avid football fan, but he may have come up with this alternative image anyway for describing his work as a therapist.

Not all coaches are people we want to identify with, but there are certainly some outstanding ones. Generally, the image of coach is a good one to use in thinking about some of what we do as pastors. Good coaches are well connected to their teams and know the strengths and liabilities of their players. They are interested in the lives of their players, not just in their athletic skills. They can see the bigger picture. They can look at the field from the wide-angle, more distant perspective. They also know the playbook. They have studied the dynamics of the game and the moves of the opposing team. They have a sense of the whole as well as the individual parts.

Of course, our work as pastors is not about sport or games or competition, so the image doesn't work completely. But it does work well to describe the kind of collaborative relationship that pastors can have with their parishioners in this work, the effort at developing personal skills, the clear sense of who is responsible for what (for example, coaches on the sidelines and players on the field), and the respect we give to parishioners for their ability, indeed the necessity, to do their own thinking and their own work out on the field of play.

The term *coach* challenges the "star," or personal charisma, elements in some versions of ministry. In the coaching image our parishioners are their own stars; they are the heroes of their own stories. We are not their rescuers or saviors. We do not make things happen for them or do things to them; rather, we simply work with them in accomplishing their goals of being people with a mission as well as living a better life and having better relationships. If their goal is to grow into sainthood within their everyday lives, then we have some ideas on how to move in that direction and can work with them to pursue it. Along with our faith and Christian teachings, family systems theory is one of our best resources for such work, and it also shows us how to function as their coach.

THE PASTOR AS FAMILY OF ORIGIN COACH

People want to make a difference. They want their lives to count for something, and they want to live a good life. Of the many arenas in which they can have this effect, family life is one of the more neglected ones. We all know the importance of family, but we have not always done a good job of negotiating its challenges. Some people—generally those from better-differentiated families—do a good job almost innately, but it is work for nearly all of us.

I don't want to make a focus on the family in church life into an idol. Family life is not the be all and end all of our faith. We in the church, and many pastors, can be too family-centered and family-focused. As Jesus pointed out on several occasions, family can get in the way of living a faithful life. Indeed, differentiation of self as a personal goal will help Christians put their family into perspective. The Gospel narratives show how Jesus differentiated a self within his family and kept his family relationships in perspective. He corrected anyone who proposed that living for family was what life is all about. Family is a primary training ground for being able to live an adult, mature, healthy life in the world. It is a good foundation for Christian mission in the world, but our family is not our mission. A healthier family makes for healthier Christians, but Christians move out beyond family in fulfilling their calling. And healthier pastors can help bring this about.

As pastors we have a resource in family systems theory that will allow people to use their own wisdom, develop their own skills, and become the heroes of their own stories. We can provide the equivalent of a locker room, a safe, calm place where we can think with them about what is happening out on the field and make plans for how to move in their lives. We can help people reconnect with the generations that have preceded them and overcome the reactivity and cutoffs that have led to poorer health for many. By virtue of their own growth, they will become resources to their own families as well as in their other communities.

Coaching church members around their family of origin issues can help them to do what healthy families have done down through the generations. Pastors have continual access to members in their church. Very few professions are allowed the access to family homes and their emotional life that pastors have. But we do need to be careful in using this privilege and in talking about family issues. Be careful not to become a pursuer by pushing people to talk about their families.

The good coach has to know the game; the best coaches have also played the game. Before becoming a coach for others, we need to have made considerable progress in doing our own family of origin work, reconnecting with others, and resolving our own triangles and our own unfinished emotional issues. We shouldn't ask others to do what we have not done.

We don't have to have had therapeutic training to do this work with parishioners. However, we do need a personal working knowledge of family systems theory. We should be able to maintain a more objective and neutral stance with regard to our own family and the families of others. We have to know how to recognize triangles and how not to get caught in them. These are the requirements for any emotionally mature person to be a coach, whatever the person's training or background. Add some solid life experience and a certain maturity of years, and many of us can become a pretty good family systems coach.

In addition to knowing family systems theory, we need the kind of personal and systemic skills described in part two—or at least have made some pretty good headway in developing them. Pastors have to know how to listen to parishioners' painful stories of family betrayal, abandonment, and significant losses without becoming anxious, taking sides, or behaving in a way that leads to even greater losses. We need to help people emerge from these stories with a sense not only of survival but of courage, mastery, and transformation. Pastors do this best when they have done it themselves.

No matter how negative the initial stories about parishioners' families are, we can help them to begin to reconnect and find ways to honor their family emotionally and to have a more positive legacy to pass on to their children. Researching their family history will help them begin to discover the wisdom and courage of former generations. They may find, unexpectedly, ways that God has been present and active in their own history. And they will gain hope and understanding for facing the challenges of their own life and have new ways of responding to them.

Coaching is about helping people to understand and change their own functioning in their most important relationships. This includes all of their relationships, inside and outside of family. As adults people usually find their own nuclear family to be their most challenging emotional relationship, but—because they are immersed in it daily—they are usually too fused into it to have a more objective perspective for changing their part in it. So, given a choice, I prefer to focus on the family of origin rather than the nuclear family. That is where it all began for them, and any progress they make there will reflect well on their efforts in their nuclear family.

BEING A COACH

In congregational ministry it can help to develop basic family diagrams on as many church members as possible. Doing such diagrams with parishioners helps them to get a new perspective on family as well as reveals what they don't know. These diagrams would be a great pastoral resource for the pastor at the time of family celebrations, such as baptisms and marriages. They would help us know who would be affected and the possible issues involved, for example, at the time of death. We would tell people this is why we wanted the information. This would also send a quiet message to our members about our interest in their own connections with family. We should ask them if we can keep these diagrams on file for future pastoral information when needed. They may want copies of the diagram for themselves.

We must build a relationship of trust with parishioners that will allow us to ask further questions about their family in later conversations. Many people, when we ask something they don't know, will get the information and bring it back to us. They will become more interested themselves and may reconnect with family members from whom they have been more distant.

We do have to remember that people are not always eager to talk about their family life and that we all have secrets we will not reveal to anyone, which may lead us to be cautious. That is fine. We should go only as far as the parishioners allow and be sensitive to their sensitivities. They will at least know of our interest in one of the most important emotional areas of their lives. At some point they may turn to us when these relationships become critical.

This information has to be given in full confidentiality. It only goes as far as us. We don't blab what we have learned about people's families to others in the church, in any context, for any reason. We don't use the information to try to make other church members aware of or sensitive to the struggles of the person who has told us about his or her family. We don't repeat anyone's own family story to anyone else without permission. And these stories most definitely should not become sermon illustrations.

We certainly don't want church members, after such a pastoral visit, to say to themselves, "Why did I say all of that about my family? What is the pastor going to think of me now?" and then distance from us. We have to stay sensitive to what it is like for them once they do begin to open up about their family life. Being open about our family to anyone outside of the family can produce feelings of major vulnerability. For some it may feel like a betrayal of their family. So we must demonstrate full care and respect when asking our questions. Even in my counseling work, I would ask counselees if they are "OK" with telling me this information about family. Remember that the feelings people have about their families are also what they tend to feel about themselves. Before I did this work, I thought of my family as pretty "messed up" and felt that this reflected on me. I didn't like to talk about my family. If a pastor had asked me about them, I might have distanced from the pastor.

Once people feel safe and trust us, they may well seek us out and want to go further on these family issues. They may see us as a resource. This is ideal, since they are pursuing us rather than our pursuing them.

When people begin to pursue us for information about family systems theory, then they are in a teachable place. If we are pursuing them, no amount of teaching will work. Whenever they bring their family situations or ask for information, we can show interest in whatever they bring and respond to their concerns. By asking them questions we are also attempting to widen their perspectives and begin to demonstrate the complexity of systems thinking and how that differs from conventional approaches.

Another way to respond is to recommend reading. An article by Bowen (see his book in the bibliography) will work for some people. Others may respond to more popular writing. Roberta Gilbert's book *Extraordinary Relationships* may be good for some people. I wrote my little book, *Family Ties That Bind*, specifically for people who were ready to begin learning about how their personal issues fit into the larger family context and what steps to take in doing their own family work.

PARTICULAR CONCERNS
AROUND COACHING CHURCH MEMBERS

We need to be aware of several concerns when becoming involved with parishioners and their families in more depth. One major concern has to do with the possibility that family of origin work, whether done in groups or individually, becomes the latest "in" thing, something that the "in" people in the church do. If this begins to happen, then we can only lightly make fun of the idea that this is happening and do our best not to promote the "movement." The creation of "in" and "out" groups is totally against what this work is about, but it could happen, at least superficially. Pointing out that a triangle is involved (the theory and the work in one corner, "those in the know" in another, and "those not in the know" in the third) can help as people learn about the mechanisms of triangles.

Also, we can count on the fact that parishioners will start to use these ideas in their own family of creation or in their workplace or with their social group or in their church relationships. While there is nothing inherently wrong with that, and it is definitely one goal of the work, it may begin to change the nature of our relationship with them if they involve us as their coach around these other relationships. Then we are moving more into the area I would consider to be "counseling," which involves another whole set of issues that are outside the parameters of this book.

Remember that the church members' relationship with the coach is not the primary one. Their focus needs to be on the family relationship system, not their relationship with us. We must make sure that our own narcissistic needs are not being indulged in the coaching relationship and that we are not allowing emotionality to build up and intensify the relationship. We want enough of a relationship so that openness and safety exist but not so much that people become emotionally attached and dependent on us and avoid doing their own work. If people are becoming too dependent and too focused on us, we must ask ourselves whether we are doing something to encourage that. How might we cool down the relationship without damaging their sense of self?

Transference is a powerful phenomenon in all relationships. Pastors are a prime object of positive or negative transference for parishioners. If they have a negative transference to us, we shouldn't even try to work with them as a coach. But a positive transference can be equally problematic. We can become too important to them. The emotional closeness of the normal counseling relationship can stimulate fantasies in them that make us into something other than their pastor. We may become their guru or the object of their romantic life.

Handled properly, the coaching relationship can avoid any heightening of this transference dynamic and avoid what happens in typical counseling relationships. However, if there is a needy part of us, if we have not worked at the resolution of our own family work, and some part of us enjoys and welcomes their positive transference, then we and our parishioners are headed for serious trouble. To nurture this kind of relationship begins the "abuse-of-power" process that is contrary to true ministry and can lead to serious misbehavior. The idea of "coach" helps us and them to keep some emotional distance so that we don't become overly important to the people with whom we might do family work.

As a coach our focus is on our parishioners and their relationship to their family. We must keep directing their attention to this focus through our questions and interest. We are just sitting on the sidelines; they are out on the playing field making their moves. They will come into the locker room from time to time to talk with us about how it is going and what changes to make in how they are moving on the field so they can achieve their goals. We have some wisdom, some ideas and thoughts to share, and some knowledge of how things work in systems, but they execute the plays. It is their "game," not ours. We have our own work to do and don't need to take on theirs. And we have no emotional stake in how things go for them and whether it goes or not. Whatever happens, we just bring our curiosity and our neutrality. We are not even cheerleaders in their corner rooting for them. To do this would potentially get us caught in a triangle.

COACHING AND FEELINGS

Remember also that family of origin work does not focus on eliciting feelings from church members. I never ask, for example, "How do you feel about that?" The expression of feelings is a tricky issue in the coaching process. Normally we feel close to anyone with whom we can openly express our feelings, indicating a certain degree of safety. Church members will express feelings in the coaching relationship because of the nature of the material being discussed. That is automatic. But as the coach we should not focus on heightening or developing those feelings. I rarely comment on such feelings or direct attention to them.

When we or our parishioners make feelings expressed to us a primary focus of the work, we increase the potential for difficulties around transference issues in the relationship with us. Expressing these feelings makes the relationship with the pastor too important. Parishioners' relationships with their family members are the important thing. It is easier for parishioners to relate to us than to their family (because they may see us as sympathetic listeners), and we need to gently keep the focus on the family system. By doing this we can avoid a lot of the usual difficulties related to the transference phenomenon. Another way to play down this dynamic is to space out appointments to once a month or more, for example.

Coaching is about thinking things through, not providing the "relief" of catharsis. We do not tell the members to stop expressing these feelings. We just give them a tissue (if the feeling involved is sadness) and ask a question that elicits more thought. Later, when the tears have dried, we can explore the connections behind the content being discussed, the tears, and the members' place in the family process and attempt to get a more objective sense of them.

Feelings and emotional expression belong within the family or relationship context being discussed. Feelings reflect people's position in their family system and are a part of those relationships "out there" on the field of action. Church members need to be able to reflect on the context in which those feelings are being experienced and ultimately decide how they want to be within that context. Keeping a low level of anxiety in the coaching session and a higher level of thoughtfulness, again without saying outright that this is what we are doing, is how we will be the best resource to members for their subjective feeling life. Being a comfort in times of upset is definitely acting as a short-term resource to people, and one not to be avoided, but helping members view the upset in a larger perspective and understand how they want to manage self within it is being a larger and longer term resource for them.

As people do their work and begin to change their position in the system, I guarantee their feelings will change. However, feelings tend not to change when they are made the focus of the work. Such a focus tends to anchor the feelings in place and solidify relationships as they are. As coaches we simply accept whatever expressions of feeling emerge and keep our focus on the context and the process. Members will slowly catch on to this interest and gradually lose their desire to rehearse old feelings with us.

COACHING AND TRIANGLES

A sure sign of a too-involved relationship, one in which boundaries have been crossed, is when the coach is becoming positively or negatively reactive to church members and their issues. If the coach is starting to think about things to do for or to the parishioners, how to fix them, change them, or somehow "get" them, then the coach is in the relationship. If the coach's own fantasy life is being stimulated and he or she is spending free time thinking about the parishioner, then this must be discussed with a consultant. The coach is getting caught in his or her own unresolved attachments, or in triangles in the family or perhaps in the church. We should ask ourselves whether we are becoming more important to the members than their family is by virtue of the intensity of our relationship with them.

We will likely have contact with other family members, and we must expect triangulation to happen from some quarter. It is automatic for members to want to triangle with the coach. This is to be expected and definitely should not be criticized or even commented on. Such attempts at triangling may come in the form of making a bid for emotional support or for taking the side of the member against another family member or, perhaps, a church member. It is up to the coach to be able to manage self within this process and not focus on getting members to stop. This is where doing our own family work around triangles is critical.

Another way to tell if we are in a triangle is if we are working harder on behalf of members than they are. I never put more energy into people's work than they do. I don't try to convince them to do it, tell them to "try harder," give them assignments, or anything like that. If they have the energy for the work, I will be there with them, but I will not be more invested than they are.

Another triangular relationship is peculiar to pastors. If we, as the coach, are also the pastor who preaches the Word of God on Sunday mornings, we will have to find a way to detriangle ourselves with the members and God so that what we say in the coaching session is not experienced in the same way as what we say in the pulpit. No clear technique for this exists; each coach has to handle it differently. Things will be imputed to us simply because we are pastors. That is part of the automatic transference that goes on around clergy all the time.

This is not a ministry of exhortation. As coaches we do not preach "family" and tell people what they "should" do. We start where they are and just "come alongside." We come with our interest, curiosity, and questions rather than telling them directly what we believe. It is a process of mutual discovery guided by our understanding of how emotional systems function.

We can get ourselves out of the "I know the Word of God about you and your family" position by the expression of our own befuddlement, either with examples from our own life or with regard to members' predicaments. We might say, for example, "I have no idea what you should be doing in this situation, but I am sure looking forward to how you work this one out. I think it will be a help to me in some of my own work." We are not there to be a person with the answers around the content of their issues; we just know something about how systems operate and how to move within them through being a researcher and asking questions. What specific stance members take is up to them.

I love using personal examples, but I tend not to use them early in the coaching process because people may take them as *the* way to do things. They can be useful later when members are not setting us up as an expert on their life. We are just a person like them, making our own way through life as best we can. Sometimes we can use examples based on how others have managed similar situations. But here we must be careful about issues of confidentiality. We must have specific permission to share a story from someone else's life.

The trickiest part of the triangular relationship for coaches may be how to be part of the normal political process of church life. *Politics* is not a pejorative term for me; it simply refers to the business of making decisions and recognizing that different people will have different opinions and will have more or less influence on how decisions get made. To be a coach of someone who is also a part of that political process—on our board, for example—requires making some distinctions and being clear about our own functioning in each context. It doesn't matter whether we agree or disagree with church members. In either case the situation is still tricky. We always have to be aware of the members' larger emotional context as well as our own personal agenda within the church. This can be done, but it has to be done with as much awareness as possible.

Unlike the therapist-client relationship, which normally has no other community connection, this pastor/coach/board member relationship is rife with potential difficulties because of the dual relationships involved. In the ideal family relationship members can pursue their own individual beliefs and purposes and still stay connected with others, even when they are at odds politically. But that is much harder for families when, for example, they run a family business together. Decisions will be made about the direction of the business that promote the ideas of one family member over another. Some parallels exist between being an executive in a family business and being part of running a church. It helps if everyone can maintain a kind of lightness, even around serious issues. This is do-able in the church, but we must pay attention.

We must not confuse family systems theory with politics or think of it as an alternative or substitute to the political decision-making process in the church. These are two separate and legitimate processes. This is where people who want the church to be "one big happy family" get in trouble. From this perspective, the church is not a family. I believe that knowledge of family systems theory makes us much better politicians. We will be smarter in our politics as we learn the theory. But such knowledge is not a substitute for the political process. Families do not vote members in or out of the family, hire and fire staff, or pass or reject certain agendas or budget priorities as we do in the church. The family business has to decide: Is it primarily a business or a family? Then, how can we still do both, but be clear about how priorities will be decided in both cases and not mix up the two ways of relating to each other?

Finally, it is important for us as coaches to stay in touch with our own coach and to have some kind of regular contact with that person. If we are working with church members around their family issues, having our own consultant is essential. Here we can continue to present our own personal work, situations from our being a coach in the church, or work with particular parishioners. I can't imagine being a coach and not having such a relationship.

Ideally, we will also be a part of a group of pastors who are meeting regularly and thinking about family systems issues in the life of the church and in our ministry. Such a group can also be a place to talk about our coaching issues as well as a place to present our own work in our family of origin. Listening to other pastors present their thinking and work on these issues is a major resource for our own thinking and work.

A FINAL WARNING

Just to be absolutely clear, these points need to be restated. We must not attempt to be a coach with parishioners in our congregations unless:

we have engaged in a serious and lengthy study of family systems theory concepts and can make use of the concepts with a relatively high degree of sophistication;

we have had at least four to five years of working with the concepts in relation to our own family of origin and have made significant progress in addressing our own unresolved family attachments;

we have a regular, ongoing relationship with a family systems theory consultant with whom we discuss not only our own family work but issues related to being a coach within our congregation.

These are minimum standards for being a family systems theory coach with our own parishioners.

12

RUNNING FAMILY OF ORIGIN GROUPS IN THE CHURCH

FAMILY OF ORIGIN GROUPS IN THE CHURCH

In addition to using coaching practice to gain a general pastoral awareness of church members' family context and to approach counseling with parishioners, a few pastors may want to take their coaching practice a step further and introduce church members to doing their own family of origin work in a small group context. This idea offers many rich possibilities for parishioners' growth and for the enhancement of church life in general, but it also presents some significant difficulties.

Not many pastors will have the time required to run this kind of group. In addition, there are particular difficulties unique to the congregational setting that make these groups into an extra challenge with a few inherent dangers. These dangers were discussed in the previous chapter and the warnings I give there must be heeded. If there is a pastoral staff along with a head pastor, it may be more appropriate for groups to be led by one of them. Indeed, the best solution might be to hire an outside professional who is proficient in family systems theory to run a church-based family of origin group.

I have to admit that I'm fascinated with the idea of a congregation in which a majority of the members, or at least the leaders in the church, have done a significant amount of their own family work. I doubt that such a church would have any fewer disagreements or differences in managing its congregational life, but I would expect the members to handle their differences in a more emotionally mature way.

As a side note, I believe that a good case can be made that the healthiest congregations have a larger percentage of their membership, and particularly their leadership, who are well-connected with their own families of origin and are better differentiated within their families. This would make a great research project. We don't have any way to do an objective test for level of differentiation as yet, but it could be possible to set some more objective standards about the number of cutoffs and the percentage of living family members people have regular contact with, as well as the number, frequency, and intensity of symptomatic issues in the congregation, in order to evaluate part of this idea.

This chapter discusses how to start and run family of origin groups in the church and how to manage some of the difficulties. Again, remember that pastors must have had extensive experience with the theory, be doing the work personally, and be having ongoing consultation with their own coach before leading such a group. We have to focus on our own development for a significant period of time before coaching others. Generally speaking, I think four to five years of consistently doing one's own family work and studying the theory is required before a person is ready to begin coaching others.

Pastors who have had previous experience in counseling or growth groups need to recognize that family of origin groups do not function in the same way. Family of origin groups do not focus on group relationships or "processing" them. Rather, the focus is entirely on learning the theory and managing self within each person's own family of origin. Of course, group members must develop trust in one another and in the leader/coach, but this results from the overall experience.

Many years ago, as I was shifting my theoretical orientation as a pastoral counselor from an individual model to family systems theory, I found myself running both therapy groups and family of origin groups. In one case a number of my therapy group members also did a family of origin group. As we compared notes after the formal ending of the groups, we all decided that the family of origin group was by far the more helpful experience. From then on I stopped doing group therapy.

INTRODUCING THE IDEA OF
AND RECRUITING FOR THE GROUPS

Although there are many ways pastors may introduce the idea of having family of origin groups in the church, what follows is how I did it as a pastoral counselor. At the time, our pastoral counseling agency ran a number of educational and growth groups for the larger community. I decided I wanted to see what it would be like to do this with a family of origin focus.

What I offered had two parts. Part one was a single-day event designed to introduce the concept of the importance of family in our current daily experience and to introduce the possibility of recruiting people to do family of origin work in a group setting. This event was open to the first twenty people who applied. I ran it on a Saturday from

9:00 a.m. until 4:00 p.m. I will describe the exercises and the process for this one-day event below.

Part two was an actual family of origin group. Open to just eight people, this group ran for nine months, meeting for three hours twice a month, in the evening from 7:00 to 10:00. Clearly, this group required a major commitment of time from the participants. I was paid to run this group, but not all pastors may have this kind of time available. Certainly, other time formats could be considered.

FORMAT FOR PART ONE

I had two goals for the day of part one: (1) to demonstrate experientially how unresolved emotional attachment in our family of origin can stay with us as adults, affecting our contemporary life and relationships, and (2) to introduce people to the idea of family of origin work.

We always ran our workshops in a local church. After registration I began the day with a brief, fifteen-minute talk about the purpose of the day and something about Bowen family systems theory. In addition, I said there would be two parts to the day: first, a few exercises to elicit some of the participants' experience in their own families, and second, my presentation of some information on doing family of origin work. I also strongly emphasized that no participants had to do any exercises that they didn't wish to and that there would be no questions asked if they refused to do them. After questions and discussion we went into the first exercise, which was usually quite powerful for people, despite its simplicity. It involved the primary triangle in all of our lives: the parental triangle.

We all went to the church gym, where I had set two chairs about ten or twelve feet apart in the center of the gym. I asked people to imagine that their mother and father were sitting in those two chairs. They were to silently position themselves in relation to the chairs based on who they were close to and distant from through most of their growing up.

As an example I showed how I would position myself to the chairs with a short explanation of why I chose that position. The participants were to wander around the gym, go out to the corners, and go up close to the chairs and between them, until they found a position that "felt right." I gave people a lot of time to do this, and I said that anyone who didn't want to do it could just sit down at the edge of the gym. Once they were in their positions I asked them to assume a stance—whether standing or kneeling, arms out or folded, turned to or away from the chairs, with any facial expressions that would fit—that would further portray their own orientation and attitude within the relationships.

Once everyone had found a place and a stance, I asked them to sit down where they were. Then, asking for volunteers, I said, "Who would like to tell us about what they went through in this process and what their position means?" People were always eager to talk about what happened to them; for some it would be an emotional experience. I asked a few questions of each person. If participants became highly emotional, I attempted to bring them back to a discussion of the relationship rather than "being in the feelings right now."

There was not enough time to hear from everyone, and I took only volunteers. I never, in this setting, directly asked a specific person to tell us what his or her experience was. The participants' silence was respected. If time allowed, I asked, "Does anyone else want to talk about his or her experience in the exercise?" The point was to demonstrate the power of the parental triangle, not to have all of the participants explain their own experience.

After a short break we went to the next exercise, which was difficult for people in a different way. I said I wanted them to take a few moments to think about and then to become their same-sex parent. I wanted them to wander around the room, introducing themselves to one another as if they were that parent, and to say some things about themselves and their relationship to their children. I demonstrated this, as an example, by becoming my father. I generally gave people about ten minutes to do the introductions. Then we talked about them in the same way as with the first exercise. After this I did a little anchoring exercise to get everyone back into their own skin and out of their parent's.

The last exercise before lunch was an introduction to drawing a family diagram. I asked everyone to draw their family diagram using the normal symbols for men and women and relationships. I usually had a handout on this, but I would also demonstrate it again with my own family. I wanted people to draw their immediate family of origin, their parents and whatever siblings they grew up with, and then any grandparents and aunts and uncles they were close to or involved with in growing up. The diagrams did not have to be complete. I told them we would be doing something with these diagrams after lunch.

After the lunch break I asked whether anyone had any comments or questions. Then I asked them to take the family diagram they had drawn and to draw a strong, thick line between themselves and whomever they were closest to in their family. Then I asked them to draw a zigzag line between themselves and whomever they had the most conflict or the biggest difficulty with.

Then I did a very brief talk about triangles and suggested that these lines might say something about their own family triangles. The strong, thick lines were probably people whom we were most likely on the inside position with in family triangles, and the zigzag lines were usually about the outside position of someone in those triangles. Then I would have people pair up in dyads and ask them to talk with each other about their lines, why they drew them as they did, and what was the family experience that led them to do it this way. Again, people were free to opt out of doing this.

I gave them only about twenty minutes in their dyads. I was not looking for a complete discussion of the relationships here but only to have some experience talking about their family relationships with another person. I brought them back into the plenary group, and again I asked if anyone wanted to talk about this exercise. If you do this workshop with people in your church, it will be quite interesting to you to hear what they say about their family triangles. It may tell you something about your relationship with them and how your own family triangles interact with theirs.

During all of the exercises throughout the day, I was paying attention to two things: first, whether anyone was getting into some emotional difficulty that I needed to be aware of. If so, it may not have been appropriate for them to continue with the day. They would decide whether to continue or not, but I would try to step aside with them and talk about that option. If they decided to drop out, then I would try to schedule a meeting with them as soon as possible after the day's event to talk with them about their experience and how they might proceed with it, if at all. Actually, I have never had this happen, but we need to be ready for the possibility that it might.

Second, I was thinking about whom in this group I might want to see participate in an ongoing family of origin group and whom I would have questions about their participating. I will explain the criteria for this later, but generally I was interested in people's level of objectivity about family and how easily they could step out of their reactivity. How defensive were they, and to what extent were they comfortable with their own underlying vulnerability and anxiety?

After a break following the triangle exercise, I gave an audiovisual presentation on a person's family of origin experience. I am aware of two sources from which you can buy or rent tapes. One is the Bowen Center for the Study of the Family in Washington, D.C., and the other is the Menninger Institute, now located in Texas, which has some excellent instructional videos (see the appendix for contact information). You may know of other sources. The point is to let the group participants see something of what family of origin work is like and what it might involve. At this point, I preferred not to present my own family work.

The concluding discussion focused first on the tape participants had just seen and then on the whole day's experience. I addressed any questions people still had about the ongoing family of origin group. Finally, I ended the day with a meditative period while I played a tape of the Mike and the Mechanics song "Living Years." Afterward, I posted a sign-up list for anyone who wanted to continue this experience by joining the family of origin group. Of course, just the day event could be presented, with no ongoing group to follow, but some resource should be made available for people whose issues get stirred up during the day.

SCREENING FOR THE GROUP

I had a half-hour meeting with everyone who applied for the ongoing group so that we could interview each other. This step was critical. At the full-day event I said that this would happen and that I would take the first eight people who seemed appropriate for the group. At that time I gave some of the general criteria, as described below.

In the interview I made sure applicants were clear about the purpose of the group. I wanted to get a sense of their own motivation for joining the group as well as a sense of what was going on in their life currently and to what extent their agenda was really more about some current issue in family that might more appropriately be dealt with in counseling. If people's current lives had significant stress, they may not have had the emotional space needed for doing this work, and I discussed this with them openly. Ideally, people would select themselves out of the group and agree that counseling (or doing nothing) would be more appropriate. They also had to know that there would be a fair amount of reading to do and that there would be a family systems theory presentation and discussion component to the meetings as well as presenting their own families.

Confidentiality is absolutely essential in the groups. No group member tells anyone else's story outside of the group even without using names. However, I always warn people that, while 95 percent of the time this standard is respected by group members, I cannot guarantee it. If a participant seriously wishes that no one else will ever hear about their family story, they should probably not participate in the group.

As I did the interview I was also trying to assess each person's level of maturity. I didn't want highly reactive people in the group, people with a great deal of unresolved family fusion, or people who were trying to deal with some immediate sense of pain and damage, who had an agenda around some current "wrong" in their family, or who were really wanting to deal with a nuclear family issue. Simply asking people about the nature of their current contact with their family of origin members was a good way to assess their level of maturity and reactivity. If they could talk about their family members in at least moderately balanced terms, had some level of perspective on the family as a whole, and were not heavily into blaming any particular family members, then they might be good candidates for doing more work on themselves within a family of origin group.

I was looking for relatively autonomous participants who would not get into significant emotional difficulty in the process of doing the family work. It is not that these people can't do family of origin work and profit from it, but they would not do best in the group context and would need to move more slowly and would have more issues to deal with along the way. They were like the people I would normally work with in my counseling practice, for whom more time was needed to prepare for doing family of origin work. I also had to have a sense that I could trust participants to honor the need for confidentiality. Certainly, those who had the most emotional maturity to begin with would do the best with the work in a group setting. Those who had less would take longer, and it might not make sense for them to be in a group.

We must carefully assess whom we are willing to work with as their coach in a group setting. We are not obliged to take all comers. Be particularly careful in working with people who really are not ready to do family of origin work. We may want to have a few counseling sessions with people to see if they can get to the kind of emotional place I describe above. If people can't begin to approximate the readiness issues described in chapter 6, then the group family of origin work will not be useful at this point.

We should not even consider offering this kind of work to parishioners who are significantly reactive and have difficulty maintaining decent relationships with others, whether with friends or with family. Until these people have adequate development and more control of their own reactivity, contact with family members may only make things worse rather than better. In most cases, people who are not ready for this work self-select themselves out of going further with it.

Also, if we have some reactivity of our own to particular people who want to do the work, then we have to avoid being their coach until we have worked on our own reactivity. It will be an unhappy experience for all if we don't do this. Usually, if we have been working at our own family issues, this will be less of a problem, but not always. If we take on people whom we know we are reactive to, we will probably exercise our issues on them.

PART TWO: GROUP FORMAT

This is the format I used when we met twice a month, three hours at a time, for nine months. At the first meeting of the family of origin group, we started off with general discussion about the process of getting to the point of doing this group. Again, I was getting a clearer sense of people's motivation and clarifying what the process was and was not about. Then I did a little talk on Bowen family systems theory and how family of origin work fits in with it. I discussed the reading and both the theory and the family presentations.

I explained that everyone would do a theory presentation and that we would have an hour for this part of the meeting. I have found that it works best to have group participants, rather than me, present theory. They are better engaged with the theory at the time, and I often learn something from it as well. It is a good way for people to clarify theoretical issues. Generally, we held twenty to thirty minutes of discussion after the presentations, usually with handouts. I stayed out of the discussion until about the last ten minutes. I would have been making notes and would step in to clarify any theoretical issues that the group may have gotten wrong or were unclear about.

I handed around a sign-up list for doing the theory presentations. On it was a list of the eight Bowen theory concepts with a date for their presentation. We would complete these presentations within the first five months. Obviously, some people would have to be ready to do a presentation early on—whoever went first would have only two weeks to work on the presentation. It worked best if I could get the first one or two people to volunteer for these first presentations so that the last person to get the list did not get stuck with the first date. People were free to trade around dates and topics if they wished. This project got them involved with the reading early.

I then did my own family of origin presentation. In this I tried to model a general presentation. I used either a large piece of butcher paper (my preferred way of doing it) or an overhead projector for showing my family diagram. PowerPoint was an option for people if they could arrange for and set up everything that was needed and were clearly proficient in its use. I preferred the large sheet of butcher paper in smaller groups so that all the names and dates were large enough that everyone could see the whole diagram clearly. It worked less well to have the diagram in bits and pieces on different screens, between which the presenter had to flash back and forth.

In this presentation I also wanted to start training participants for their part in the group process of asking questions in response to each presentation and not making interpretative comments. In this way we were starting to work on the research stance and helping the presenter to think more about family. This step also usually required some clarifying of what real questions are versus the "Don't you see how . . . ?" type of question that is really an interpretation.

Then I handed around a sign-up list for everyone to present their family within the first five months of the group. We scheduled one family presentation per evening. Again, I tried to get volunteers for the first two meetings before handing around the list. I also repeated the warnings about confidentiality at each meeting.

The last four months of the group were more loosely organized. Everyone would do a follow-up to the family presentation, usually in the order of the first presentations. They would discuss what had happened in their work since their last presentation and would get more questions from the group and discuss how they would proceed. I did some additional presentations either on the theory or on the processes of doing the work. We also had lots of general discussion about family work. People were free to offer "case examples" of their use of the theory, if they wished.

Finally, I want to say a word about timing. If my obsessive personality has not already become clear by this point, be certain that I was a stickler for time. I always started and ended at the agreed-on time, and I didn't let presentations run over. I believed it was important for people to know just how much time they had and to be able to count on that. These were long evenings, and people needed to have a sense of their time commitments, without worrying that they would end up going a lot longer than expected.

The theory presentations ran for an hour total; the presenter could take up to thirty minutes, but it was essential to have group discussion on each concept and not let the presenter talk for the whole hour. Family of origin presentations would last ninety minutes. People could take up to an hour to present their family and then we had thirty minutes for the group to ask questions and for the presenter to respond. It was important for the group to practice asking systems-oriented questions rather than to speculate, in general discussion, on the issues in a person's family. This skill of developing greater objectivity and being curious about family process would further aid their own family work. Again, I usually came in later in this process with my questions. I would also take the privilege of making comments about any theoretical issues involved at the end of the presentation.

13

ISSUES AND CHALLENGES
FOR THE PASTORAL COACH

I was having breakfast in a restaurant one Saturday morning when a man and a young boy came in and sat down in front of me. I quickly assumed that he was a "Saturday Dad," spending the day with his approximately six-year-old son. Whether this was true or not, the man immediately opened his newspaper and held it up in front of him, blocking a view of his son. The boy was silent for about a minute and then he picked up his knife and began to lightly tap it on the table. Then he began to hum quietly. The tapping and humming got steadily louder, and still there was no reaction from Dad. After hitting a crescendo the boy stopped and sat quietly for about ten seconds. Then he said, "Daddy, don't you like me?" I just about fell apart in tears but kept watching. The man got the point, put down his paper, and began to try to interact with his son.

Then I began to imagine what might happen when this boy grew up, assuming the distant relationship with his father did not change all that much. The grown man might have difficulties with depression and self-esteem and become an underfunctioner in his marriage. His wife then would encourage him to "go talk with the pastor." Among other issues and discussion, the pastor could ask, "Tell me about your father." The man might well say, "He never liked me or wanted much to do with me. My parents were divorced, and he never showed much interest in me. We have just sort of drifted apart over the years, and it has been a long time since I last saw him."

Assume you are the pastor in this story. How would you proceed? And in particular, what might be your stance with regard to this story about the man and his father? In addition to the discussion in part two about doing family of origin work, here are a few extra things to think about as a coach. I will go through these points in no particular order.

COACHING FOR DEVELOPING THE RESEARCH STANCE

Generally, people have certain set beliefs about their family when they start this work. As coaches we don't directly challenge their beliefs, but we do want to get them questioning and wondering. For example, we don't know whether what the man says about his father is true or not. Our only goal is to encourage people to think more clearly and objectively about family and family processes. By asking questions we invite skepticism about their old beliefs and assumptions. We draw their attention to the gaps in the stories with our questions and to the things that just don't add up. Through this process, we are encouraging them to be curious and to move toward the research stance. It is good practice to ask systems-oriented questions that stimulate interest rather than defensiveness or guilt.

We don't bludgeon anyone with this idea. If people defend against a question and don't answer it, don't try more than once more to ask it in a different way. It just means we have touched on something they are not ready to think about. If we try to argue with them or convince them that this is something they should think about, it won't go well. Remember that their "resistance" is also about our impatience and our pushing them to get something. We are helping to create the resistance. Give up the pushing or pulling. We can instead let go of our end of the rope and move on without comment.

Let's say that the man also had what he described as "a critical mother." He said that she never seemed to get off of his case. He said the same thing happened in his marriage; he just never seemed able to do anything right in the eyes of his wife. When people are describing the negative behavior of others toward them and we have explored the interactive process involved, we should ask something like, "Do you know what your best method is for getting this behavior from them?" or "If you wanted to get that behavior from him right now, what would you have to do?" They often say "What?" but then, as they think about it, the question becomes clearer. We hope that people will catch on that it is an interactive process in which each person plays a part. Thinking about these things, the man may begin to question his sense of himself as a victim simply at the mercy of others.

We don't *make* others behave badly toward us, but we play a part. Do we know what it is we do? Let's assume the man agrees to go visit his father and mother and to work at trying to reconnect with them. If people are going to be making a family visit in which this negative behavior could happen, I ask, for example, "What are the chances that you will do something in this visit that will get your mom to be critical of you?" And then, "Will this become a justification for distancing from her?" Or, "What would it be like for you to not do it?" Or, "If you decide to do it, then what would it be like to move toward her, in a nondefensive way, with interest in her reaction to you?" Or, "When you are with your dad, what would you have to do to convince yourself that he was not interested in you and didn't like you?"

I like "What would it be like . . . ?" questions because they don't tell people to do anything; rather, they simply explore possibilities and raise options to think about. These subjunctive mood questions usually reveal more about the interactive process and the anxiety of the people doing the work. They invoke our ability to play-act or to imagine a scenario without actually committing to do it. Sometimes I precede the question with a kind of nonpursuing phrase, such as "I don't think you should do this, but I was wondering what it would be like if. . . ." Other phrases like this include "I know this sounds crazy . . ." or "This is probably the wrong direction to go . . ." or "Let's play with this idea in our imagination . . ." or "I know you really can't change your feelings with him, but what would it be like for you if . . ." or "I don't think I could do something like this but . . ." or "Here is another one of my crazy ideas; what would it take for you . . . ?"

I directly discourage people from talking about their feelings with other family members in this work. Doing so will only revive old circular reactive processes. It might feel good at the time, but it doesn't usually lead to anything positive. The point here, at this stage of the work, is to get to know our family members and to have a clear sense of how the family has functioned emotionally in terms of systems theory; it is not to have them understand us. At some point people may reach the goal of a one-to-one relationship which has give-and-take in mutual understanding, but that will take time. It is not the starting point of the work.

Assuming the research stance and maintaining it will change the nature of the interaction with others. Genuinely wanting to understand other people's experience of their life and being interested in the emotional functioning of the family system creates a new experience. For some people this feels inauthentic and "not real," meaning it is not how they usually behave in the family. I suggest to these people that they admit, only to themselves, that they are "pretending" to be the best researcher they can conceive of. After a while, as they begin to learn things and see the value of this way of functioning, it will no longer feel phony. As we learn to see things differently, we will come to different conclusions about our family and ourselves.

My wife, Lois, once took a drawing course based on the book *Drawing on the Right Side of the Brain*. It challenged her to actually "see" things differently. The premise was that we draw what we "think we see," not what is actually there. We draw our image of a horse, not the actual horse. So the book suggested exercises such as drawing the "negative space"—the area around the horse—or drawing the image upside down. These exercises made her look more closely at how things actually are and at their relationship with one another, rather than at how she

thought they were. She was able to see the actual proportions and relationships among individual elements much more accurately. This is like
the research stance. When we go back to family with a focus on what we
think we know, then we stay stuck.

In attempting to get to know both of his parents better, the man in
our earlier example may discover something of what it was like for them
growing up in their families. He may hear some of his own words being
used to describe how they felt and what they experienced with their parents. He will get a better sense of what they were up against. Listening to
their stories will put a new perspective on his experience. He will begin
to understand that the family story is not just about him, that a multigenerational process has been going on for many years. He will begin to
see how he may transmit his earlier perspective to his own son or daughter if he doesn't start making some changes.

THINKING THROUGH OUR SELF-DEFINITION

A major piece of differentiation of self is thinking through our own
beliefs, commitments, values, and life principles. This can include our
beliefs on a grander theological scale. It will also include our general
goals in life, what kind of a person we want to be, and the kinds of values
we want to uphold. What is our own sense of purpose or calling in life?
What are we willing to dedicate ourselves to? The coach will have occasion to raise these kinds of questions with people.

More particularly, this self-definition involves specific acts of how
we will and won't be within certain kinds of relationships and circumstances. Preceding the issue of "how" to deal with it when our mother
complains to us about our father is what do we believe about this? What
do we understand to be happening? What do we believe we can and can't
do about this situation? What do we think is "right and good" behavior
in this circumstance? What principles have we adopted that will guide us
as we respond?

Thinking these kinds of things through is just for ourselves. We
don't broadcast them to other family members and try to convert them
to our way of thinking. We don't even try to state them or explain them
to others. We just act on the basis of our beliefs. Explaining or reasoning
with others will usually get us caught up in the emotional process again.
The others will have to do their own thinking about these issues for
themselves, or not. Our assumption of an "I position" will challenge
them to arrive at their own.

THINKING TRIANGLES AND REMAINING NEUTRAL

In being a coach we have to *always* be thinking "triangles." Even when supervising very experienced counselors and ministers, I see how easily they can be caught in triangles and begin to see things as their counselees see them. If our questions or comments tend to focus more on other family members, from the same point of view as the people we are talking with, then we are probably in a triangle with them. If we are joining in with a pursuer to pursue a distancer, or to get an underfunctioner "to be more responsible," or to get someone to "open up" or "shut up," then we are in a triangle. We are no longer attempting to expand an understanding of "the problem"; instead, we have become a part of the problem by pushing a particular solution.

Let's say you have invited the wife of the man in the earlier example to join the counseling sessions. She assumes she is there to help you help her husband. The therapeutic triangle is then focused on him. She is ready with a list of things the two of you need to focus on to fix the husband. If you had difficulty with your own critical mother, you may either react to her angrily or not feel up to "challenging" her by pursuing an interest in her own issues and their history in her family. You may cooperate with her deflections back onto her husband.

If we have a tendency to lose the systems focus ourselves and shift over to an other-focused individual model along with our church members, or to step into their triangles, it may help to keep a copy of their family diagram on our lap and to keep looking at it. Doing so may help us to remember, "This is about the family system, not just the person in front of us."

We have to remain neutral around family issues and avoid colluding with the people no matter how "just" their cause sounds. The best way to be on their side is to be on everyone's side. This is another way to think about being neutral. Neutrality is not about having no opinion or beliefs of our own. Indeed, it may even be useful to have some personal sense of how we might behave in the circumstances. However, such private thoughts are only for us; they are not to be taught to the counselees. Remember that "the process is the content." Our focus is on the functioning of this emotional system, not the arguments the counselees use to justify their positions within the system.

Side-taking is about trying to make things safe for ourselves. It is a normal process, but we have to move beyond it. Again, I never declare to people, "I don't take sides." It sounds very self-righteous and off-putting.

Just don't "be" on a side. And even though parishioners may resent at the time that you are not more sympathetic to their "cause," they will appreciate it later. We want to look at everyone's part in the family emotional process and see how each person contributes to keeping things as they are. Changing an issue is not of fault-finding but of taking responsibility for one's own part in a process and changing only that.

Anything we pastors say about other family members who are not present can and very well may be used by parishioners in their own triangular and reactive stances. They may repeat our words—or, more often, some more negative interpretation of our words—to others. If other family members think we are seeing them negatively, then we are caught in the family triangle whether we want to be or not.

One woman wanted to talk about her marriage, and her husband would not come in despite my making a phone call to him (which usually brings the spouses in). She complained constantly about his "paranoia" and major, angry reactivity. She had been to see a psychiatrist who, sight unseen, had labeled him as "paranoid" and then referred her to me. She had repeated the psychiatrist's diagnosis to him, and the husband assumed I would have the same stance. I began to tell the wife that I didn't think she understood her husband very well and that she needed to get to know him better. And I told her to tell him what I said. She was hesitant to repeat these less flattering words (about her) to him, but I insisted. He eventually began to get this message from her and liked that I had said she didn't understand him. Finally, he came in for marital counseling with her. I got myself out of that triangle, and we were able to move ahead.

If we as coaches get caught in our church members' stories and their way of seeing, then we can't be of value to them. We have to remember that the content and feelings involved in their stories are about their position in the triangles. If we lose sight of this, we are caught in their family triangles with them. We have to remember that their patterned way of knowing is only part of the facts. Maybe even some "facts" are wrong and have to do more with their emotional reactions to events. Our questions, based on an understanding of the theory and of the functioning of their emotional system, are an effort to open up new ways of seeing and understanding the facts.

To further illustrate this, I sometimes propose the "Nine-Dot Exercise" for trainees. I put nine dots up on a whiteboard and ask people to connect them all with just four straight lines without lifting their pen from the paper (see diagram on next page).

Unless they know the "trick," they realize it can't be done in the way they are thinking of the dots. This well-known exercise illustrates in-

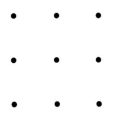

the-box thinking. People, in their minds, automatically draw a line around the outside of the dots and create a box. They don't go outside of the box. They are not seeing things as they really are; they have added something to the "facts." The solution involves going beyond the imagined boundaries.

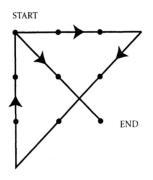

Other than as a general principle, I don't tell individual people, "You are not seeing things as they really are." They will only become defensive in response. Their perceptions, thoughts, and feelings are shaped by the triangles they are in. I want them to discover this on their own as a result of their asking questions in the family and reflecting on their part in the emotional process. My questions help them to suspend their "knowing" and to start researching the way things really are. We have to ask a lot of questions, preferably about things they have never thought to ask. Once they become curious, we can then ask, "How could you go about finding out about that?"

Being able to engage in the research stance is the key to beginning this work. We have to be able to maintain the stance ourselves and model this curiosity in our way of being with people. If we slip into the people's own family experience and become other-focused with them, then we are not serving as a resource. When I am feeling stuck with a person or I have run out of questions to ask, I ask myself, "What am I not focusing on or paying attention to here?" Often I am in an unrecognized triangle.

PATIENCE, PACE, AND PLANNING

Patience is another key to being a coach. People have to move at their own pace in this work. Athletic coaches are famous for pushing their teams to excel in dramatic ways, but this will not help in family of origin work. We must respect people's fears and hesitations and not try to move them beyond their own felt limitations.

Once people have begun to grasp family systems theory concepts and have developed a calmer, more objective picture of their family, feeling more in charge of their own reactivity, they will be able to develop their own pace for making differentiating moves in their unique family system. The flow of their work will be mostly up to them, with us acting as a consultant/coach. We will have to be monitoring our own anxiety as we watch and respond. Are we getting anxious about their work? Is this about some unfinished work of our own? I can become anxious around people who have a higher level of differentiation than I do and who are ready to tackle more than I would be. I just have to sit back, watch, and learn, and often be amazed at their ability to move in a system and at their grasp of what is happening. If I let my anxiety interfere, they could be held back by it.

A significant potential for abuse of group members exists in any group. As coaches, if we push people to do work they are not ready for or to see a situation as we see it, then we are verging on abuse. We must pay attention to our urges to make something happen with people in our group. That is not our job, and such urges must be coming from something in us. If we start to push people, they may be compliant or rebellious, but it will not go well. The group members will see this and have difficulty trusting us. They will be more hesitant to present their material. They will feel less safe.

The same goes for the other group members. Group members can also forget to be researchers and start trying to persuade people about what they "should" do. Then they can get resentful if a person does not do or want to do what they say should be done. This is really off base theoretically and totally against the spirit of a family of origin group. We do not "require" people to do anything, nor do we "psychologize" people's "resistance." I actively intervene if I see this happen.

I also avoid telling people what to do in the early stages of their family work. They are usually anxious enough just about moving back toward family in a different way. I don't want them to be anxious about dealing with me and my suggestions too. As people become more comfortable and demonstrate that they can easily think for themselves and evaluate my ideas in terms of how they fit for them, I may share my thoughts and suggestions directly. When they are less dependent on me and no longer treat me like an authority figure, we can have a good coaching relationship.

If we are working with people in a group setting, then planning for reentry into the family is done as a part of that experience, and others get to learn from it. Ideally, people come out of their family presentation with a better sense of the family emotional process and what their part in it is. Along with the group, we will have raised questions for them, such as "What will it take for you to get to know your father better?" or "What have you learned from your mother about her depression, and how could you learn more from her?" or "Who would have been closest to your dead grandfather and known him the best? Could you approach that person for more information on him?" or "How do various members of your family handle anger? Which parent might be willing to talk with you about his or her experience of anger in the parent's own family? What if you went to that parent and said you are having trouble managing your own anger? Could he or she help you?" There are, of course, thousands of questions that can be raised with people and serve as the basis of a reentry plan.

Much of this work is about people discovering their own courage, but they have to arrive at it for themselves. I can clearly remember how scary it was for me to send that first letter off to my mother asking about my father. One man who also had a relatively benign mother that he had difficulty moving toward called me at my office from the airport to say he had just let his plane take off without getting on it. We had done a lot of work on this first visit home after many years of distance and on the few questions he might ask. But it was too scary for him. He took the trip in another month's time, and then he wondered what he had been so afraid of. But he had to know that I was OK with whatever he decided to do. If I had given him a "pep" talk or told him what he "had" to do, then he might have dropped out entirely from the effort or gone and made the visit, complying with my expectations, but then blown it somehow. When he told me, I just gave a light chuckle and said, "Oh yeah? Tell me what that was about." People become their own heroes in this work, and they learn to feel better about what they can do emotionally.

Our job as coaches is to provide a safe atmosphere in which people can just be, think, and make plans they are comfortable with. If they don't accomplish their plans, that is fine too. Something also can be learned from that. It is our role to just stay curious. They are taking on scary and difficult work, and they must not be criticized in any sense if they hesitate or appear to fail at it. They are simply doing what they need to do. If we attempt to do anything to get them moving or be anything other than a safe, less-anxious presence, then we are reacting and over-functioning, and that is our own family issue.

If we have expectations of them, this will most likely lead to their distancing in some form. This is the "back pew" phenomenon. They will feel our impatience. The more we are just a researcher interested in whatever is happening, or not happening, the more they will take responsibility for their lives. The man in our opening example would be quick to hear our impatience as criticism. But if we are easy with however he decides to be, he may slowly begin to realize he really is in charge of his own life. Then he may begin to find the courage to make moves in relation to others that he would regard as risky.

On the other hand, we can't let their fears control our curiosity. Remember, we are dealing with two forms of anxiety. There is the anxiety that goes with reactivity and that inhibits us from acting and keeps us stuck. We can explore this with people and learn from it. And there is the anxiety of growth. Growth anxiety occurs whenever we want to try out some new behavior that we have determined we want to do but, because it is new, we just don't know how it will go or how we will manage. It helps to clarify this type of anxiety with people and to let them know that new behaviors will almost always be accompanied by some anxiety. No one does this work calmly and easily.

What we as the coach have to distinguish is the kind of anxiety people are dealing with and, in either case, not be infected by it ourselves. If people are too afraid to make new moves, are we being affected by that fear as well and being too cautious? On the other hand, might we be thinking they are not ready when in fact they are? If we have dealt with these different kinds of anxiety in our own family work, we can probably make the distinctions needed with them. We have to remain objective in being able to evaluate the risks for people and not encourage them to take on more than they are able to do or to hold them back from doing what they are able to do. We have to decide in our own mind whether they are being too timid, or too reckless, and understand our own reaction to that. This awareness requires clarity about the history of their own emotional functioning in their family and the kind of personal resources they have to draw upon.

We need to have a clear sense of the toxic or difficult issues that people face in their families and of how everyone in the system has behaved around these issues over time. For church members to address these issues with differentiating or detriangling moves, or even just to research them, requires some careful planning. Can they anticipate the likely reactivity of the people involved? What might be the larger family emotional process? What will they do when or if other people do their typical moves in response? Will they move ahead or back off? Will they retreat to a safe place and reconsider? How will they handle the reaction if they move ahead? How will they manage their own anxiety as they continue on course with their plan and not collapse into the resistance of others to their being a more solid self? What emotional reaction from others is likely to cause them the most difficulty? What is it, in particular, that makes that reaction from others so difficult for them? How will they deal with it? What will they say or do? If they were tempted to relent, what would they most likely do? How might they lose it totally and blow up or run away? If they succeed in holding to their plan initially, how will they maintain it over time and how will they relate to the people involved? Are their expectations about the outcome of their moves and what they will produce too high? Have they done enough research around all of this so that they can predict who will have what reactions? These are just some of the typical planning questions we can ask.

Finally, remember that this work is not primarily about giving or getting "forgiveness" in the family. Forgiveness is a very tricky issue, and we can disguise a lot of emotional process behind it. Forgiveness can sometimes imply a one-up or one-down relationship that simply doesn't fit with a system analysis of the situation and that will only continue the emotional process in place. Usually, as people do their work, this issue just dissolves or evaporates. Of course, some issues simply do involve forgiveness, but I wouldn't rush to assume that right off the bat. My own stance is that it is God who forgives and that it works best if we just try to understand how things came to be as they are and what our own part in them might have been.

14

THE BENEFITS OF DOING FAMILY OF ORIGIN WORK

Doing family of origin work does not solve all of the problems of life. It does not bring to an end the emotional pain and challenges that family life can sometimes produce. People who do the work may still divorce, have trouble with their kids, and disagree with their parents or siblings. A church whose members have done the work will still have conflicts and differences. These things are a part of normal human life, and we will not put an end to them in this world. There will be lots of room for personal growth and development and things to learn and master even if much of our family work is accomplished.

But doing our family work gives us a real leg up on all of these issues and makes them easier to handle emotionally and not be so anxiety provoking. For me, it has been one of the most useful and meaningful experiences of my life, second only to my conversion and growth in the Christian faith. Family systems theory generally, as well as my own family work, has done more for my relationships with others, and particularly with my wife, than anything else I have done. Personal friends and colleagues who know the theory, and most of the people I have worked with, would probably divide their lives into before and after Bowen theory.

I am not a rah-rah person. I like balanced, realistic, nonidealized pictures of things because I know that there are no perfect solutions to life's challenges. Anyone who knows me, as my wife does, knows I have a lot of room left for personal growth. But I do want to finish this book with some positive comments on the benefits that I and most other people experience as a result of doing family of origin work.

1. First, we have a sense of being more in charge of our own life. This is the experience of being less reactive to the thoughts, feelings, and behaviors of others and being more proactive instead. We take more personal responsibility for how things go in our life and spend less time blaming others or cursing our fate. We have much less of a sense of being a victim of others and more of a sense of choice in how we relate to others apart from how they relate to us. Most people who do the work arrive at an experiential equivalent of Paul's words to Timothy: "For God has not given us a spirit of fear, but of power and of love, and of a sound mind" (KJV).

2. We experience a greater acceptance of self as we are. We have a comfort with self in both our limitations and our strengths as well as much less anxiety about how others see us. Learning Bowen theory has deepened my understanding and experience of God's grace.

3. We accept what has not been a part of our family life that we wish could have been. I think of this as the experience of emptiness that many of us desperately and vainly try to fill. People try to fill this inner emptiness with relationships, status, accomplishments, material things, work, and drink or drugs or other addictions, but those things don't and won't do it. I believe the experience of God's grace in doing this work allows us to become more comfortable with this inner emptiness and just accept it.

4. Family systems theory and family of origin work offers us a realistic hope for growth as individuals, and as families, and for our churches. It is not based on false, impossible, or idealistic expectations. It is straightforwardly honest in how difficult the work is and how short most of us will come in relation to what we would like to achieve in becoming more differentiated people. Hope for improvement and for further mastery of self's part in the challenges of life helps keep us going. The theory gives us a realistic basis for that hope of achieving our goals.

5. Doing this work gives us a clearer sense of love as something that we do and give to others, rather than as something we don't have and have to get from others. In the Bible, love is nearly always an action rather than a feeling. Person after person has discovered this along with a stronger sense of compassion for what others have suffered. I find a strong ethical dimension implicit in Bowen theory that comprises a part of what differentiation of self involves. I have also found in the theory a means for better accomplishing the values I believe in as a Christian and that I want to uphold in my life.

6. Many people discover a clearer sense of their own convictions and beliefs and a willingness to stand for them nonreactively in the face of opposition. All the people I have worked with through the family of origin process have arrived at wanting to talk about their faith even though they did not come in to see me as people in search of faith. I have not introduced the topic. It has resulted from their work as they have tried to clarify the beliefs and principles they will live by. This is an essential part of differentiation. This work evokes a desire for faith and of courage in holding on to our beliefs.

7. Finally, in terms of community, the theory provides a solid experience of the organic body of Christ, close and connected and yet with each part different. Paul's image in Corinthians of the body consisting of many diverse parts but still working together for the good of the whole is epitomized in the theory. People discover experientially what unity in

diversity can really be and how we can be closely connected with those we differ from significantly. Paul's most distant future perspective on the eschatological horizon is of a time when "God will be all in all." Bowen family systems theory moves us in that direction.

I return to the sailing image I used in chapter 1 and to Michael Kerr's comment that working on differentiation of self is like taking our little boat out into the lake on a stormy day. In doing so, we hope to learn more about storms, about ourselves, and about how to manage ourselves in the midst of the storms. Each day of ministry can introduce us to new kinds of storms and situations for which we could not have been directly trained. We need to have the skills that differentiation of self offers and learn to master our little boat in the midst of the turbulent storms.

We want to learn how to relate to the most intense experiences of our lives, during times of higher anxiety in our families, in our churches, and in our world, and be able to steer a course that we have chosen based on our own beliefs and principles. Rather than staying in a safe harbor, where nothing is ventured or learned or gained, or crashing on the rocks, where all is lost, we can learn to move in a self-determined direction in cooperation with God's Holy Spirit.

This image immediately evokes for me the account of Jesus, Peter, and the disciples on the stormy lake. The truly nonanxious presence of Jesus in the midst of the storm could have lowered Peter's anxiety as he stepped out of the boat into the chaos of the violent waves. But taking his eyes off of the goal, reverting to his old way of functioning and fusing with his anxious imagination and fears, he began to sink.

Healthy churches require healthy leaders; they require people who can function well in the emotional storms of life. Bowen theory offers a means for doing family work for all pastors and church leaders that leads toward that goal of greater health. The work will lead to lowered anxiety and better functioning in almost every aspect of our lives. All who do this work will improve their leadership in the church and take others into a more profound experience of faith simply by virtue of their own greater emotional maturity. We grow by learning to embrace and honor our own people and be curious about their stories. As we let go of the need for them to be different from how they are and teach ourselves to be less anxiously connected to them, we will change. Even though they may also resist the change that comes with our greater differentiation of self, they also will grow and change, becoming healthier family and church members together.

APPENDIX

Here are several resources for finding either a coach or audiovisual materials.

1. The Bowen Center for the Study of the Family, found on the Web at www.thebowencenter.org. This center, founded by Murray Bowen, is considered the primary source of definitive information on family systems theory. The center may also be able to connect you with related centers in other parts of North America. Contact them by mail at the following address:
   Bowen Center for the Study of the Family
   4400 MacArthur Blvd. NW Suite 103
   Washington DC 20007-2521
   Phone: 800-432-6882

2. Eastern Seminary has a valuable audiovisual resource in tapes that were originally made through the Menninger Clinic. I have used several of these tapes and found them very informative for both lay and professional audiences. The Web address is: www.ebts.edu/Library/AV_collections/video_counsel.htm.

3. Many seminaries and freestanding groups run training programs for clergy in family systems theory. The number of places seems to grow daily. I recommend one group in particular: Leadership in Ministry, directed by the Rev. Larry Matthews. This group offers residential, three-day workshops, held in five different locations across the United States, which meet twice a year for theory, case, and family of origin presentations. The Web address is www.LeadershipInMinistry.com. Contact them by mail at the following address:
   Dr. Lawrence Matthews
   8502 Stonewall Dr.
   Vienna, VA 22180
   Phone: 703-560-8314

4. Peter Steinke has done extensive work in the area of family systems theory and the congregation. However, I believe he focuses less on family of origin work. Type his name into your preferred search engine, and you will find many listings.

5. Look on the Web under related terms, including *healthy congregations* or *healthy ministry*, and you will find even more listings. However, the number of listings that focus on family of origin work are still relatively small. In addition, you can search the Web for other resources. When I entered the phrase "family of origin therapy" into a Web search engine, I got over eighty-nine thousand entries, some of which were relevant.

BIBLIOGRAPHY

Bowen, Murray. 1978. *Family Therapy in Clinical Practice*. New York: Jason Aronson.

Freeman, David S. 1992. *Family Therapy with Couples*. New Jersey: Jason Aronson.

Friedman, Edwin H. 1985. *Generation to Generation: Family Process in Church and Synagogue*. New York: Guildford.

Kerr, Michael E., and Bowen, Murray. 1988. *Family Evaluation: The Role of Family as an Emotional Unit That Governs Individual Behavior and Development*. New York: Norton.

Richardson, Lois, and Richardson, Ronald W. 1990. *Birth Order and You: How Your Sex and Position in the Family Affects Your Personality and Relationships*. Vancouver: Self-Counsel.

Richardson, Ronald W. 1996. *Creating a Healthier Church: Family Systems Theory, Leadership, and Congregational Life*. Creative Pastoral Care and Counseling. Minneapolis: Fortress Press.

———. 1984. *Family Ties That Bind: A Self-Help Guide to Change through Family of Origin Therapy*. Vancouver: Self-Counsel Press.

CPSIA information can be obtained at www.ICGtesting.com
Printed in the USA
LVOW12s1130301013

359258LV00004B/5/P